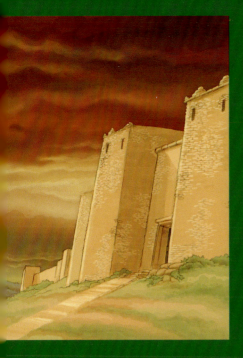

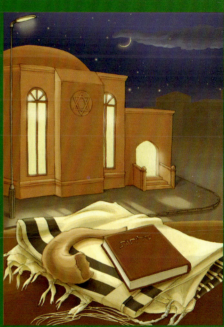

The Jewish year
Round and Round and Round and Round and Round and Round

Tamuz-Av

Round and Round and Round and Round and Round and Round and Round and Round
The Jewish year

by Tziporah Rosenberg   illustrated by Ruth Beifus

Originally published in Hebrew as
Ma'agal Hashanah (1977)

Translated by	Graphic design by
Sherie Gross	**Aviad Ben Simon**

ISBN 978-1-59826-376-3

Copyright © 2009 by Sifriyat Sharsheret

All rights reserved. No part of this publication may be translated, reproduced, stored in a retrieval system or transmitted, in any form or by any means, electronic, mechanical, photocopying, recording or otherwise, without prior permission in writing from the publishers.

FELDHEIM PUBLISHERS
POB 43163
Jerusalem, Israel
208 Airport Executive Park
Nanuet, NY 10954

www.feldheim.com

Printed in Israel

10 9 8 7 6 5 4 3 2 1

In loving memory

of the author

Rebbetzin
Tziporah Rosenberg, ע״ה

*She dedicated her life
to serving Hashem
and sacrificed for the
education of Jewish children*

*Taken from us
in the prime of her life
on 17 Adar 5758*

ת.נ.צ.ב.ה

Sefiras haOmer

Pesach has passed. All the children have gone back to school.

Chanie went happily back to school, too. What a nice classroom, Chanie thought. Everything looked so clean. The tables, chairs, blackboard and walls — everything was spotless, just like new.

There were also new pictures on the walls. How bright and colorful everything looked!

Chanie walked around her classroom and looked at all the posters. One of the posters was a round cardboard chart. There were many numbers on it.

"What is this chart?" Chanie asked her teacher.

"It's a *sefiras ha-omer* chart," answered the teacher.

"What's *sefiras ha-omer*?" a few girls asked together.

"Good question, girls," the teacher responded. "I'll tell you all about it."

The girls sat quietly and listened as the teacher spoke.

"When did the Jews leave Mitzrayim?" she asked.

"On Pesach!" the girls answered.

"And when did they get the Torah?" the teacher asked.

"On Shavuos!" they shouted.

"Right! On Pesach we left Mitzrayim, and on Shavuos we got the Torah. And from Pesach to Shavuos we have a mitzvah to count the days in between. Every day we count how many days have passed from the day we left Mitzrayim. We count with excitement until the day that we received the Torah.

"When do we start this special mitzvah of counting? On the second night of Pesach.

"During the time of the Beis HaMikdash, the *korban ha-omer* was brought on the second day of Pesach and that is when they started counting.

"And so we call this counting-mitzvah *sefiras ha-omer*, since they started counting on the same day that they brought the *korban ha-omer*.

"How many days do we count altogether? Forty-nine days, which is exactly seven weeks."

"The chart that is on the wall," the teacher explained, "shows us how many days have passed from the day of *Yetzias Mitzrayim*. The arrow points to the number that we count for *sefiras ha-omer*."

All the children stood up happily and said with their teacher,

הִנְנִי מוּכָן וּמְזֻמָּן לְקַיֵּם מִצְוַת-עֲשֵׂה, כְּמוֹ שֶׁכָּתוּב בַּתּוֹרָה: וּסְפַרְתֶּם לָכֶם מִמָּחֳרַת הַשַּׁבָּת... שֶׁבַע שַׁבָּתוֹת תְּמִימֹת... הַיּוֹם שְׁמוֹנָה יָמִים שֶׁהֵם שָׁבוּעַ אֶחָד וְיוֹם אֶחָד לָעֹמֶר!

"I am ready to fulfill the positive commandment, as it says in the Torah, 'You shall count from after the Shabbos... seven complete Shabbosos...'

"Today is eight days, which are one week and one day to the *Omer*."

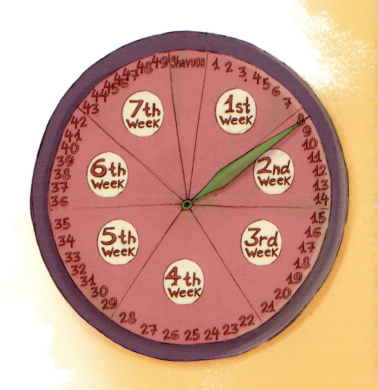

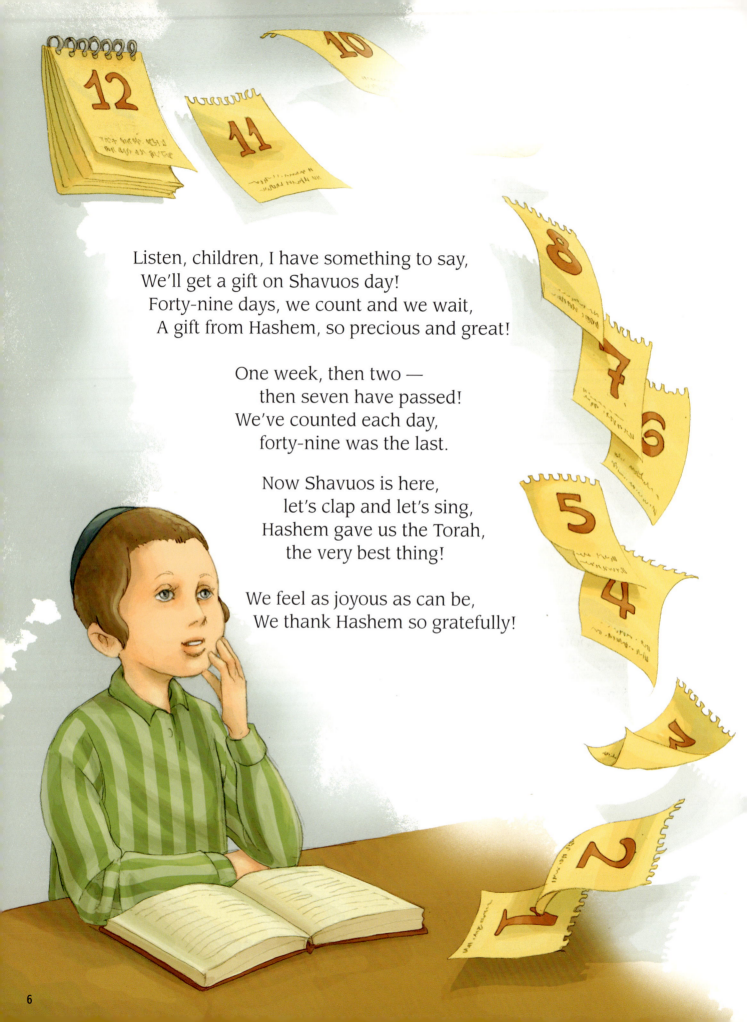

Listen, children, I have something to say,
We'll get a gift on Shavuos day!
Forty-nine days, we count and we wait,
A gift from Hashem, so precious and great!

One week, then two —
then seven have passed!
We've counted each day,
forty-nine was the last.

Now Shavuos is here,
let's clap and let's sing,
Hashem gave us the Torah,
the very best thing!

We feel as joyous as can be,
We thank Hashem so gratefully!

Korban haOmer

What is the *korban ha-omer*?

It is a sacrifice of barley that was brought in the Beis HaMikdash.

When spring comes, the fields are filled with barley and wheat. The new crop is already golden and ripe, and it seems to be saying, "Come, harvesters, cut off our stalks! The time of harvest has come!"

But, no! We are not allowed to harvest the crop and eat from it until we bring a *korban* to Hashem. We must first thank Hashem for all the good that He has done for us — for all the wonderful rain and for the fields filled with grain.

The grain gets ground into flour, and with the flour we make dough, and with the dough, we make: bread, challah, cakes, cookies and many, many more foods that satisfy us and taste delicious!

We bring a *korban* from the stalks of the new crop that we cut so that we'll remember the *chessed* Hashem did for us.

How do we sacrifice the *korban ha-omer*?

On *Erev Pesach*, the messengers of the *beis din* went out to the fields near Yerushalayim. There they tied bundles of barley stalks so that it would be easier to cut them later.

On the second night of Pesach people gathered in the fields. Three people with sickles and baskets came to cut the stalks.

They asked the others, "Has the sun set yet?" And they answered, "Yes!"
They asked again, "Has the sun set?" And they answered, "Yes!"
And a third time, "Has the sun set?" And they answered, "Yes!"

Then they asked, "This sickle?" And they answered, "Yes!"
"This sickle?" And they answered, "Yes!"
"This sickle?" And they answered, "Yes!"

Then they asked,
"This basket?"
And they answered, "Yes!"
"This basket?"
And they answered, "Yes!"
"This basket?"
And they answered, "Yes!"

If it was Shabbos they asked,
"Is it Shabbos today?"
And they answered, "Yes!"
"Is it Shabbos today?"
And they answered, "Yes!"
"Is it Shabbos today?"
And they answered, "Yes!"

Then they asked,
"Shall I cut?"
And they answered, "Cut!"
"Shall I cut?"
And they answered, "Cut!"
"Shall I cut?"
And they answered, "Cut!"

Then they cut the stalks and brought them with great happiness as a sacrifice to Hashem. This sacrifice is what we call *korban ha-omer*. ("*Omer*" is an amount of stalks.)

We hope and pray that we will soon merit seeing this great happiness in the Beis HaMikdash.

Ready and ripe,
  golden and tall,
"Come take us now!"
  the stalks seem to call.
Just wait a bit more,
  did you forget?
The time has not come,
  for harvest just yet.
First thing we do,
  is cut just a few,
A *korban* to Hashem
  to tell him, "Thank You!"
Then we'll return
  and harvest the wheat,
And all of the families
  will have bread to eat!

Mourning during Sefirah

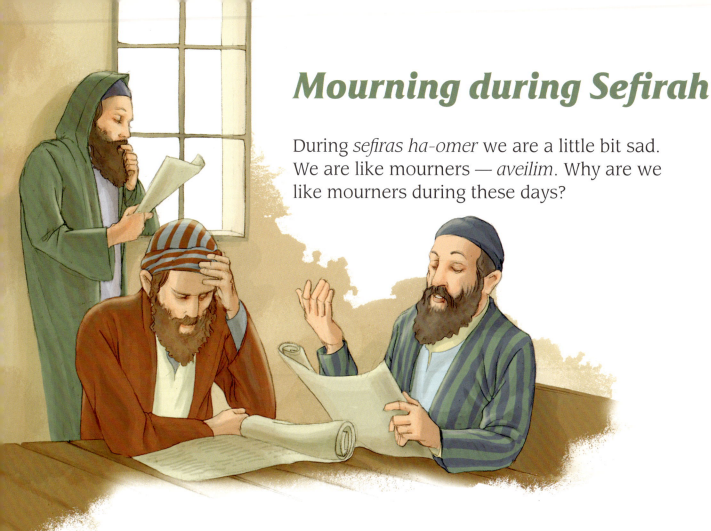

During *sefiras ha-omer* we are a little bit sad. We are like mourners — *aveilim*. Why are we like mourners during these days?

The story that answers this question is very sad.

Many years ago, there lived a very big *tzaddik*, and his name was Rabbi Akiva. He was a great *talmid chacham*, and was one of the holy *Tanna'im*. (The *Tanna'im* are the great Torah Sages mentioned in the Mishnah.)

Rabbi Akiva had many, many students who came to learn Torah from him. They came from all over, because he was very famous for his holiness and his greatness in Torah learning.

In fact, Rabbi Akiva taught thousands of students — twenty-four thousand! All of them were righteous *tzaddikim* themselves, and all of them were Torah scholars — *talmidei chachamim*.

Do you know, children, how to show respect to *talmidei chachamim*?

Talmidei chachamim are very important people. They learn Torah all the time, and it is because of them that the whole world exists.

We must show them respect by listening to them and standing up when they pass by. We have to honor them as much as we can! We certainly are not allowed to insult them or embarrass them or bother them in any way, *chalilah*.

Well, something very bad happened right in Rabbi Akiva's yeshivah. The students weren't showing proper respect to one another! Since they were all *talmidei chachamim*, they were all supposed to stand for each other and treat each other with great respect.

Then, some of Rabbi Akiva's students caught a terrible sickness. Then some more and then some more! The students got so sick that they died.

Do you know when this happened? It all happened during the days of *sefiras ha-omer*. That is why these days are sad for us. We show our sadness by not playing music, by not making weddings and by not taking haircuts during *sefiras ha-omer*.

אָמַר רַבִּי עֲקִיבָא: וְאָהַבְתָּ לְרֵעֲךָ כָּמוֹךָ
זֶה כְּלָל גָּדוֹל בַּתּוֹרָה!

Rabbi Akiva said, "Love your fellow Jew as you love yourself. This is an important rule in the Torah!"

Hashem loves us and that's why He commanded us to love each other. He wants us to be kind to each other and respect and help one another.

There are so many things we can do to fulfill this mitzvah:

Gemilas chessed — helping our friends,
Hachnasas orchim — inviting guests to our homes,
Bikkur cholim — visiting people who are sick,
Ahavas rai'im — loving each other,

and many, many more!

Love Your Fellow Jew as Yourself

Let's see how Chanie treats her friends nicely.

1. Chanie is playing ball. Her friend stands by, watching her quietly.

She invites her friend to play.

2. Oh no! Shulamis fell off the swing!

Chanie goes over to her quickly, picks her up, and calms her down. She whispers in her ear:

Are you okay?

Don't cry, Shulamis! I'll take you to your mother.

3. Look how Chanie shares with everyone!

Pesach Sheni

The fourteenth day of the month of Iyar is Pesach Sheni. What is Pesach Sheni?

During the time of the Beis HaMikdash, we had a mitzvah of bringing a *korban Pesach* on the fourteenth day of Nisan. Jews came from all over Eretz Yisrael, far and near, to fulfill this great mitzvah in Yerushalayim.

But what happened to those people who had to travel from very far and couldn't get to Yerushalayim on time? Or to those who were sick or *tamei* and couldn't bring a *korban Pesach*? What could these Jews do — did they lose out on this big mitzvah?

No, not at all! Hashem gave them a chance to bring a *korban Pesach* on a different day — all of the Jews who couldn't bring a *korban Pesach* on the fourteenth day of Nisan, brought their *korban Pesach* a month later instead, on the fourteenth day of Iyar.

Pesach Sheni is not a *Yom Tov*. On this day, we are allowed to eat *chametz*, but in order to remember Pesach Sheni, some have the custom of eating a piece of matzah.

Lag baOmer

The thirty-third day of *sefiras ha-omer* (ל"ג) is a happy day. Why are we happy on Lag baOmer?

On this day, the terrible sickness of Rabbi Akiva's students stopped.

Many of Rabbi Akiva's students had died during the first weeks of *sefiras ha-omer*, which was a great tragedy. So when the sickness stopped on the thirty-third day of the *sefirah*, everybody was happy.

We, too, are happy on Lag baOmer and we are allowed to play music, make weddings and take haircuts.

Lag baOmer Bonfires

Why do we light bonfires on Lag baOmer?

We light bonfires to remember a great *tzaddik* who brought a very brilliant light to the world. This great *Tanna* lit up the world with his Torah. His name was Rabbi Shimon bar Yochai.

Lag baOmer

Happy, happy, as can be,
Lag baOmer's on its way,
Happy, happy, as can be,
Pile the branches up today!

Lighting up the sky,
Rabbi Shimon bar Yochai!

Happy, happy, as can be,
What a *tzaddik*, oh so bright,
Happy, happy, as can be,
"Rashbi" shone with Torah light!

Lighting up the sky,
Rabbi Shimon bar Yochai!

The Story of Rabbi Shimon bar Yochai

Rabbi Shimon bar Yochai was a very big *tzaddik*. He was one of the holy *Tanna'im*. His son, Elazar, was also a *tzaddik*. Rabbi Shimon and his son learned Torah together day and night.

At that time, the evil Romans ruled Eretz Yisrael. They made many rules that were bad for the Jews and caused them a lot of suffering.

One time, the Romans decreed that no one was allowed to learn Torah! And another time, they said that no one was allowed to keep Shabbos!

The Romans were always coming up with ways to make it hard for the Jews to keep the mitzvos. And whoever didn't listen or spoke against them was punished very badly. The Jews were afraid of them and didn't want to speak against them.

One time, Rabbi Shimon sat with two other great *Tanna'im*, Rabbi Yehudah and Rabbi Yossi. They were talking about the Romans and their evil rules against the Jews.

Rabbi Yehudah said, "The Romans have also done some good things. They built markets and stores for buying and selling. They built bridges for people to pass over the rivers. And they built bathhouses so people could wash up."

Rabbi Yossi heard what Rabbi Yehudah said, but he didn't agree or disagree. He didn't want to praise the evil Romans, but he was also afraid to say anything against them.

Rabbi Shimon wasn't afraid of the Romans at all. He remembered all of the difficulties they had caused the Jews: They had burned down the Beis HaMikdash. They treated the *talmidei chachamim* badly. And they didn't let the Jews keep the Torah and do mitzvos.

So Rabbi Shimon answered Rabbi Yehudah and said, "The Romans are bad people. Whatever they have done was only for their own good. All the things you mentioned are really bad for us; the Romans didn't mean it for our good."

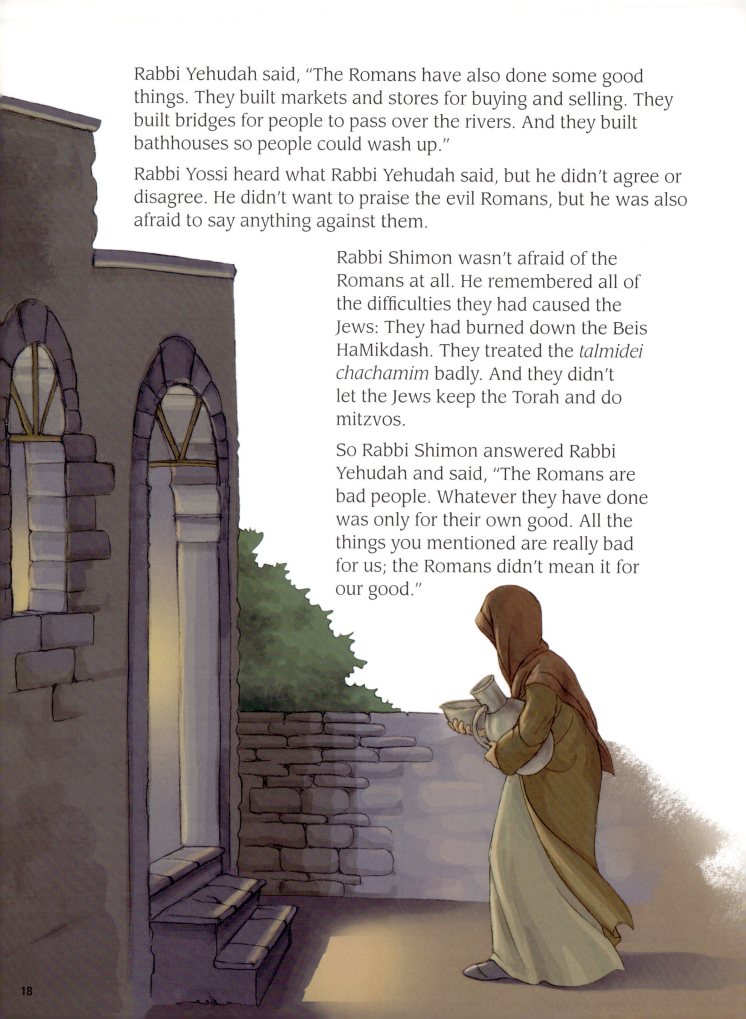

The Roman ruler heard about what Rabbi Shimon had said. He became very angry at Rabbi Shimon and ordered that he should be killed.

When Rabbi Shimon heard this, he went to hide in the *beis midrash* with his son, Elazar. They stayed in the *beis midrash* and learned Torah. They didn't go out at all, so that no one would see them and give away their hiding place. Rabbi Shimon's wife would secretly bring them food and water.

A short while passed. Then Rabbi Shimon heard that the Romans were looking even harder for him. He realized that if he didn't hide somewhere safer, they would catch him.

Rabbi Shimon and his son ran far, far away to a place called Peki'in. There they hid in a cave, and no one at all knew where they were.

But how did they have food? After all, no one knew that they were there, so no one could help them! Hashem made a great miracle for them. A carob tree grew overnight outside of the cave, and on the tree were ripe fruit!

And how did they have drink? When they entered the cave, they heard the sound of water — trickle-trickle. What a miracle! Hashem had put a spring of fresh and pure water right there in the cave!

Rabbi Shimon and his son were so happy and thanked Hashem for His kindness. They ate the carobs and drank the spring water. They realized that they had to take special care of their clothing, since they didn't have anything except what they were wearing. So they wore them only for davening. After davening, they took them off and covered themselves in the sandy ground of the cave. That is how they sat and learned Torah.

They both became very skinny, and their skin became dry and cracked. But these things didn't bother them, as long as they were able to learn Torah in peace. Nobody disturbed them in the cave, and they were able to understand things that even the greatest Sages didn't understand.

Rabbi Shimon and his son remained in the cave for twelve years! During this time, Eliyahu HaNavi would come to them and teach them secrets of the Torah.

At the end of twelve years, Eliyahu HaNavi came to the entrance of the cave and said, "Who will let Rabbi Shimon know that the Roman ruler has died and the decree has been cancelled?"

Rabbi Shimon and his son heard this and happily left the cave.

What did they see? They saw people working very, very hard. They were working the fields — plowing and planting, plowing and planting. All day long they worked very hard.

"How could people behave this way?" Rabbi Shimon wondered. "They work hard all day and don't learn any Torah!"

Then Rabbi Shimon heard a *bas kol* saying, "Go back to the cave!"

Rabbi Shimon and his son went back to the cave and stayed there for another year.

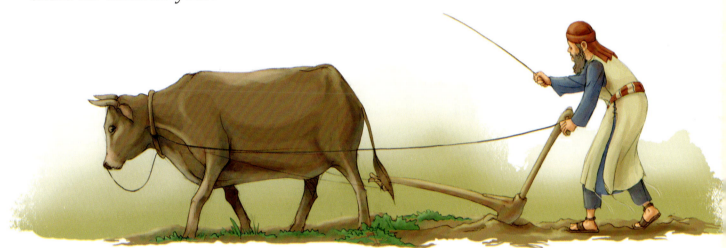

Again, they heard a *bas kol*. "Come out of the cave!" said the voice from Heaven. They left the cave and what did they see? They saw an old man holding two bundles of good-smelling *hadassim*. The man was in a big hurry because it was *Erev Shabbos* and it was late in the day.

"What are those *hadassim* that you are holding?" Rabbi Shimon asked.

"In honor of Shabbos!" he answered.

"And why do you need two bundles?"

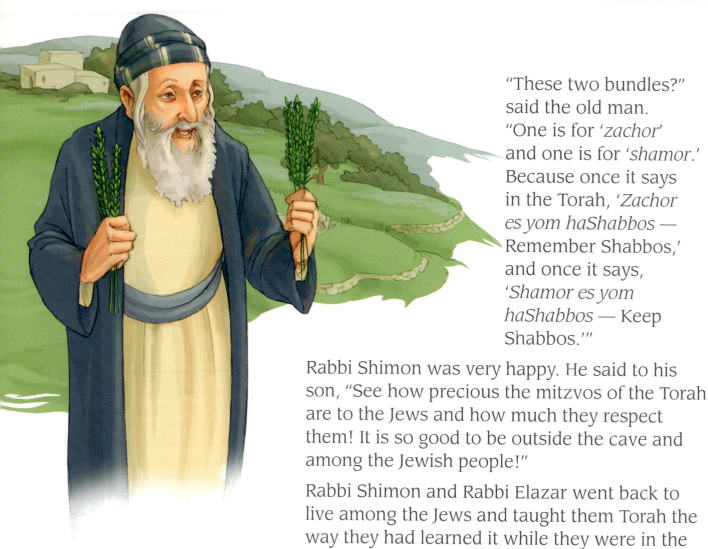

"These two bundles?" said the old man. "One is for 'zachor' and one is for 'shamor.' Because once it says in the Torah, 'Zachor es yom haShabbos — Remember Shabbos,' and once it says, 'Shamor es yom haShabbos — Keep Shabbos.'"

Rabbi Shimon was very happy. He said to his son, "See how precious the mitzvos of the Torah are to the Jews and how much they respect them! It is so good to be outside the cave and among the Jewish people!"

Rabbi Shimon and Rabbi Elazar went back to live among the Jews and taught them Torah the way they had learned it while they were in the cave. This was how many Jews began to learn and understand the Torah at that time.

In the merit of this great *tzaddik*, who brought so much light of Torah to the world, there was blessing and good fortune for all of the Jews; during Rabbi Shimon's lifetime, there was never a rainbow in the sky. This was a good sign for the Jews — it meant that Hashem was protecting them in the merit of Rabbi Shimon, the *tzaddik*.

Rabbi Shimon bar Yochai passed away on Lag baOmer. Before he died, he taught his students many secrets of the Torah. He also gave them the holy *sefer* that he wrote, *Sefer haZohar*.

וַאֲמַרְתֶּם כֹּה לֶחָי!
רַבִּי שִׁמְעוֹן-בַּר-יוֹחַאי...

A Neighborhood Bonfire

The children got together on Lag baOmer to build a bonfire.

Everyone joins in the fun of bringing the branches. But they are very careful not to take what belongs to others.

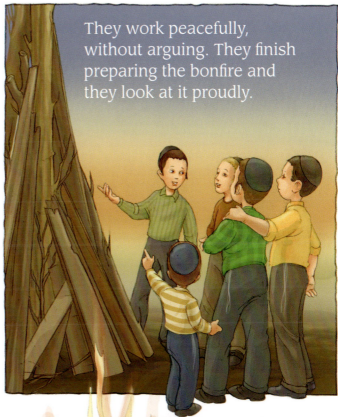

They work peacefully, without arguing. They finish preparing the bonfire and they look at it proudly.

"Be careful, children!" Yossi's father lights the bonfire. "Move away, children! It's dangerous to stay too close!"

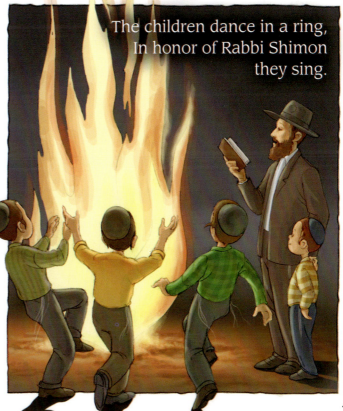

The children dance in a ring, In honor of Rabbi Shimon they sing.

Hilulah d'Rashbi

Lag baOmer is called *"Hilulah d'Rashbi,"* which means it was a day of happiness for Rabbi Shimon bar Yochai. This is because on this day he taught his students a lot of Torah!

Torah is Light

Just like fire lights up darkness, so too the Torah lights up the world. We light bonfires that light up the night on Lag baOmer to remind us of the great *tzaddik* who brought a great light to the whole world — the light of Torah.

Rabbi Shimon bar Yochai is buried in Meron in the north of Eretz Yisrael. Many people travel there on Lag baOmer. Some people light great big bonfires nearby. They sing and dance and daven to Hashem. They ask Him to help the Jewish people in the merit of this great *tzaddik*.

A Song for Lag baOmer

בַּר-יוֹחַאי, נִמְשַׁחְתָּ אַשְׁרֶיךָ,
שֶׁמֶן-שָׂשׂוֹן מֵחֲבֵרֶיךָ
בַּר-יוֹחַאי, שֶׁמֶן מִשְׁחַת-קֹדֶשׁ
נִמְשַׁחְתָּ מִמִּדַּת הַקֹּדֶשׁ.

Shavuos

Hooray! The day of Matan Torah is almost here!

The sixth day of Sivan is the great *Yom Tov* of Shavuos. This is the day that we received our holy Torah and the day that we became Hashem's special nation. We thank Hashem for all His goodness — that He gave us His Torah and that He chose us to be His treasured people.

אַתָּה בְחַרְתָּנוּ מִכָּל הָעַמִּים,
אָהַבְתָּ אוֹתָנוּ וְרָצִיתָ בָּנוּ וְרוֹמַמְתָּנוּ מִכָּל הַלְּשׁוֹנוֹת
וְקִדַּשְׁתָּנוּ בְּמִצְוֹתֶיךָ קֵרַבְתָּנוּ, מַלְכֵּנוּ, לַעֲבוֹדָתֶךָ
וְשִׁמְךָ הַגָּדוֹל וְהַקָּדוֹשׁ עָלֵינוּ קָרָאתָ.

כִּי הֵם חַיֵּינוּ...
וּבָהֶם נֶהְגֶּה יוֹמָם וָלַיְלָה

"The words of Torah are our life… and we will ponder them day and night." Torah is our life; without Torah we have no life.

The Torah is compared to water. Just like fish cannot live without water, so too, the Jewish people cannot live without Torah. If a Jew separates himself from the Torah, *chas v'chalilah*, it is as if he has no life!

Learning Torah

It is a very big mitzvah to learn Torah. We call this mitzvah *"Talmud Torah."*

The Torah learning of children is especially important and beloved. We are taught that the world only exists in the merit of the learning of *tinokos shel beis Rabban* — the children who study Torah.

עֵץ חַיִּים הִיא לַמַּחֲזִיקִים בָּהּ

It is a tree of life for those who grasp it.

לֶקַח טוֹב נָתַתִּי לָכֶם, תּוֹרָתִי אַל תַּעֲזֹבוּ

For I have given you good instruction: do not forsake My Torah.

אַשְׁרֵינוּ!
מַה טוֹב חֶלְקֵנוּ!
וּמַה נָּעִים גּוֹרָלֵנוּ!
וּמַה יָּפָה יְרֻשָּׁתֵנוּ!

How fortunate are we!
How good is our portion!
How pleasant is our lot!
How beautiful is our heritage!

Before Matan Torah

Before Hashem gave the Torah to the Jewish people, He asked all of the nations of the world if they wanted the Torah.

He asked the descendants of Esav, "Do you want the Torah?"

The people of Esav said, "What is written in the Torah?"

Hashem answered, "Do not kill!"

The people of Esav said, "No, we don't want the Torah! We won't be able to keep it, because we are used to killing people."

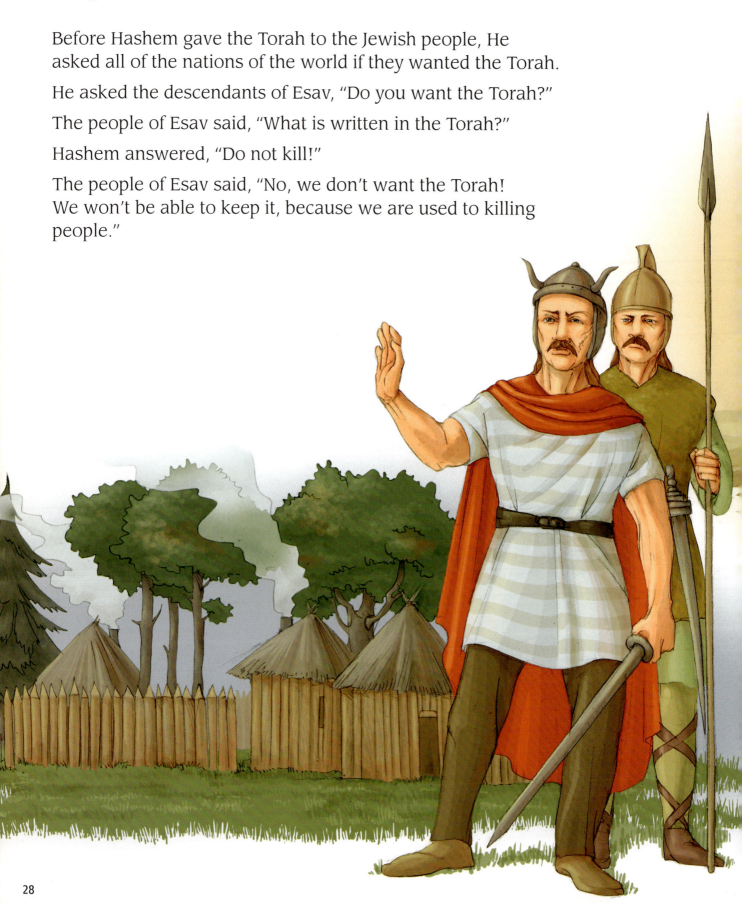

Hashem asked the descendants of Yishmael, "Do you want the Torah?"

The people of Yishmael said, "What is written in the Torah?"

Hashem answered, "Do not steal!"

The people of Yishmael said, "No, we don't want the Torah! We are used to stealing!"

Hashem asked all of the nations. No one wanted to accept the Torah because they wanted to continue their bad ways.

But when Hashem asked the Jewish people, they answered all together,

"Na'aseh v'nishmah —
We will do and we will listen!"

Har Sinai

When Hashem wanted to give the Torah
to the Jewish people, the mountains began to argue.

Har Carmel said,

"Hashem will choose me,
Since I'm handsome and tall,
He'll give the Torah right here,
Because I'm biggest of all."

Har Tavor said,

"No, sir, Har Carmel,
You'll see, I'm the one,
I'm prettier than you,
And I won't be outdone!"

Har Bashan said,

"Not on Carmel,
And not on Tavor,
I am the nicest,
Don't wish anymore!"

This is how the mountains argued with one another. Only Har Sinai remained quiet. "I am quite small," Har Sinai thought to himself.

Hashem said,

"What are you arguing about, you haughty mountains? I will not give the Torah on you, Har Bashan, or on you, Har Carmel, or on you, Har Tavor! I will give the Torah on the humble Har Sinai!"

The mountains were embarrassed by their silly behavior.

Then Hashem made beautiful grass and flowers grow on Har Sinai in honor of the giving of the Torah.

Matan Torah

When the Jews left Mitzrayim, they didn't get the Torah right away. They weren't holy enough yet to receive the holy Torah. In Mitzrayim, they had learned from the Egyptians. They had learned not to love one another, to fight and argue and to say bad things. After they left Mitzrayim, they did many good deeds. They became holier and holier from day to day.

The Jews waited for seven weeks to get their special present. When they got to Har Sinai, they didn't argue with each other anymore; they loved each other so much that they were like one person with one heart!

When Hashem saw how much they cared about each other, He said to Moshe, "Go and tell the good Jews, 'The time has come that I, Hashem, want to give you the most precious present in the world — the holy Torah! You will be My most special nation in the whole world — *mamleches kohanim v'goi kadosh* — for I am giving the Torah only to you!'"

נַעֲשֶׂה וְנִשְׁמָע!
We Will Do and We Will Listen

When Moshe Rabbeinu told the Jewish people that Hashem wanted to give them the Torah, they were overjoyed! All together they proclaimed,

"Na'aseh v'nishmah — We will do and we will listen!"

First they said, "We will do" — we are ready to do whatever Hashem says, even though we don't yet know what He will say. Then, "We will listen" — we will listen to the Torah and mitzvos.

When the Jewish people said "Na'aseh v'nishmah," they were *zocheh* to something very special. Two special crowns were fastened to their heads by angels: one for "na'aseh" and one for "nishmah."

וּבָאוּ כֻלָּם בִּבְרִית יַחַד
נַעֲשֶׂה וְנִשְׁמָע אָמְרוּ כְּאֶחָד!

**They all came together in one covenant,
"Na'aseh v'nishmah" they said as one!**

Sheloshes Yemei Hagbalah

The three days before Shavuos are happy days that are called Sheloshes Yemei Hagbalah. What is happy about these days?

These were the days that the Jewish people prepared for the giving of the Torah. Oh, how great was the happiness!

Imagine: in three days the Jews would become the chosen nation! Only they would get the special treasure, the precious Torah.

The men and the women, the old and the young, even the little children, all joyously prepared for the day of Matan Torah. Moshe Rabbeinu made a border around Har Sinai so that no one would get too close to the mountain. At the moment that Hashem would give the Torah, Har Sinai would become so holy that no one was allowed to touch it.

This is how they prepared: For three days, they washed their clothing, cleaned their homes and prepared special foods. One day passed, and another, and then the great, holy day arrived, the day of Matan Torah!

"*Va-yehi ba-yom ha-shelishi…* — And it was on the third day…" Hashem came down to Har Sinai to give the Torah to His beloved and precious nation — *Klal Yisrael*. That morning, even before the people woke up, thunder and lightning could be heard and seen. The sound of a shofar became louder and louder and Har Sinai was covered in smoke!

The Jews quickly got up and went to stand around the mountain. They stood near the fence and they were careful not to — *chas v'chalilah*! — touch the mountain. This is how they stood, in great joy, and waited to receive the Torah.

Who was standing around the mountain?

All of the Jews were there — fathers, mothers, children and babies. Even all of the unborn babies who were still in *shamayim* came to accept the Torah. Even we were all there — your father, your mother and all of you! All of us heard the words of HaKadosh Baruch Hu and all of us promised to keep them.

At that moment, in Hashem's great love for us, He healed all the sick people.

Whoever had been blind, could see.
Whoever had been deaf, could hear.
Whoever had been mute, could speak.
And whoever had been lame, could walk.
There were no headaches and no toothaches,
No stomachaches and no foot aches.
Everyone, everyone was healthy and complete.
How wonderful! Hashem loves His people so very much!

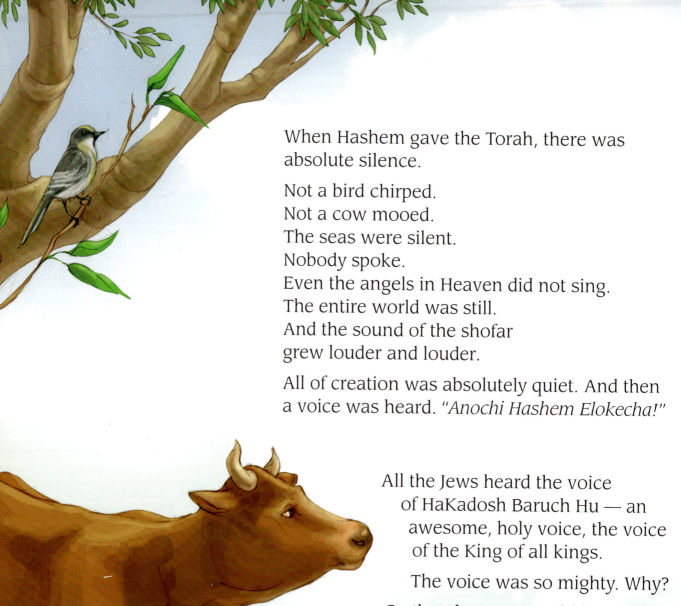

When Hashem gave the Torah, there was absolute silence.

Not a bird chirped.
Not a cow mooed.
The seas were silent.
Nobody spoke.
Even the angels in Heaven did not sing.
The entire world was still.
And the sound of the shofar
grew louder and louder.

All of creation was absolutely quiet. And then a voice was heard. "*Anochi Hashem Elokecha!*"

All the Jews heard the voice of HaKadosh Baruch Hu — an awesome, holy voice, the voice of the King of all kings.

The voice was so mighty. Why?

So that the Jews would have *yiras shamayim* — fear of Heaven, so that they would be afraid to transgress His mitzvos. This was also to honor *Klal Yisrael* all over the world. When the nations of the world heard this very mighty voice, they understood that the Jews are the most important nation in the whole world. Why?

Because the great King, Hashem Himself, had spoken to them and given them the holy Torah.

The Jews received many, many mitzvos.

There are *taryag* — תַּרְיַ"ג — 613 mitzvos in the Torah.

The Jews received all of the mitzvos at Har Sinai,
but the *Aseres haDibros* were heard by all in a mighty voice at Har Sinai.

עֲשֶׂרֶת הַדִּבְּרוֹת
Aseres haDibros

1. אָנֹכִי הַשֵּׁם אֱלֹקֶיךָ....
2. לֹא יִהְיֶה לְךָ....
   לֹא תַעֲשֶׂה לְךָ פֶסֶל....
3. לֹא תִשָּׂא....
4. זָכוֹר אֶת יוֹם הַשַּׁבָּת....
5. כַּבֵּד אֶת אָבִיךָ וְאֶת אִמֶּךָ....
6. לֹא תִרְצָח.
7. לֹא תִנְאָף.
8. לֹא תִגְנֹב.
9. לֹא תַעֲנֶה בְרֵעֲךָ עֵד שָׁקֶר.
10. לֹא תַחְמֹד....

Shavuos Customs

On Shavuos we have a custom to eat dairy food, as well as food made with honey. This is because the Torah is compared to honey and milk, as it says, "Honey and milk are under your tongue…" (*Shir Hashirim* 4:11).

There is another reason for eating dairy food. Right after the Jews got the Torah at Har Sinai, they ate only dairy food. This is because before they got the Torah, they didn't know how to prepare kosher meat. So when they learned the laws at Har Sinai, they didn't have any kosher meat to eat. To commemorate this, we eat dairy too.

On the night of Shavuos, we have a custom to stay up all night and learn Torah. Since this is the day that we got our precious present, we don't want to part from it. We learn it all night to show how dear the Torah is to us and how much we love it!

Another reason for staying up all night is because on the morning of Matan Torah, the Jews were still sleeping when Hashem woke them with thunder and lightning. We try to make up for and correct what they did by staying up all night and learning Torah with great happiness.

On the night of Shavuos we also recite an entire *sefer* called "*Tikun Leil Shavuos.*"

In honor of Shavuos, we decorate the shul with greenery and flowers, to remember Har Sinai that was filled with grass and flowers.

Before the reading of the Torah we have a custom to say "*Akdamos*" which praises Hashem, the Torah and the Jewish people.

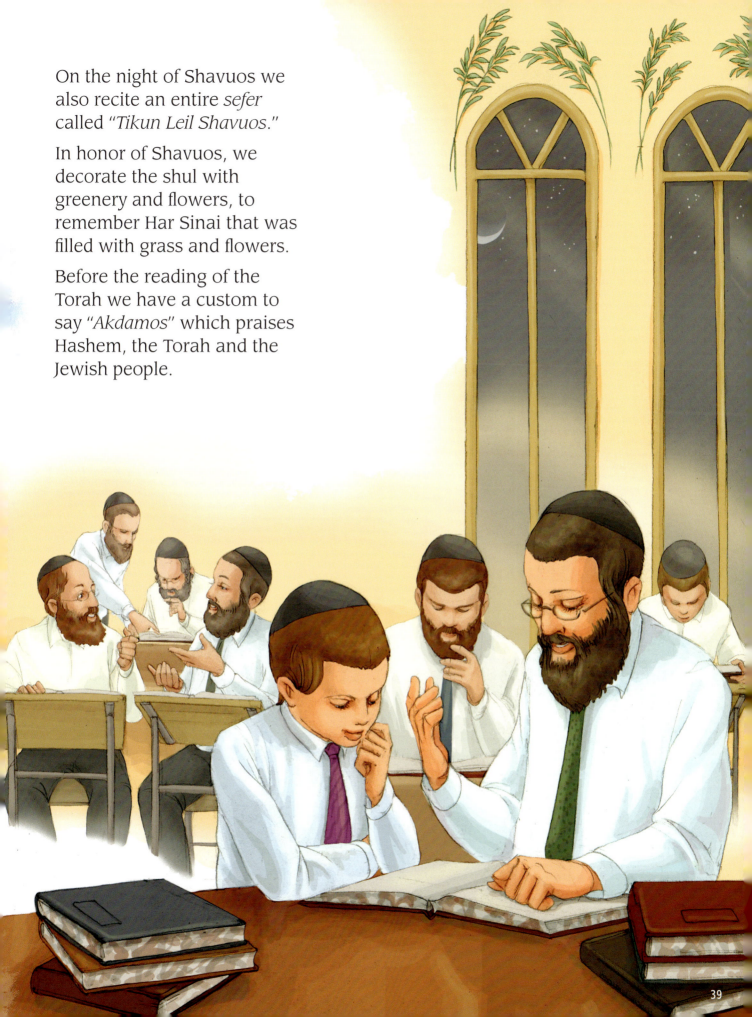

Going up to Yerushalayim

How glorious it was when the Beis HaMikdash stood in Yerushalayim!

Three times a year all of the Jews went joyously up to Yerushalayim: on Pesach, Shavuos and Sukkos. This is called *"Aliyah laRegel."* They went on foot all the way, singing and dancing and playing instruments, until they reached Yeushalayim.

The Jews came to the Beis HaMikdash and brought *korbanos* to Hashem. They celebrated throughout the *Yom Tov*. Even though so many people and children came, it was never crowded — there was room for everyone in Yerushalayim.

Bikkurim

In the days when the Beis HaMikdash was standing in Yerushalayim, we had a mitzvah to bring "bikkurim."

What are bikkurim?

The first fruits on the trees are called bikkurim. This comes from the word "bechor," which means firstborn.

The bikkurim were brought from the special fruits that Eretz Yisrael is blessed with — the shivas ha-minim.

Every person who had fields and vineyards went out to his field to check if fruit was growing. When he saw the first fig growing on his tree, or the first pomegranate growing on his tree, he immediately tied it with a ribbon so he would know that this was the first, the bechor.

These fruits would stay on the tree for a long time because they were still small and not yet ripe. When the fruits became ripe, the owner of the field went to collect the first fruits — the bikkurim — and he put them all in a basket.

How did he know which fruit had grown first? After all, there were so many fruits on the trees!

But he did know — and he found them right away!

There it was — the fig that he had tied with a red ribbon! That was the first fig. And there was the pomegranate — the one he had tied with a red ribbon! That was the first pomegranate. And there was the cluster of grapes, the one he had tied with a red ribbon! That was the first cluster of grapes.

This was the way the owner of the field collected the *bikkurim*. He put them all into a big basket that was decorated nicely, and put the basket onto his ox. The ox was also decorated beautifully in honor of the mitzvah. Then he went to Yerushalayim with great joy.

What a beautiful sight! When a group of people would walk together toward Yerushalayim, they would pass many villages and cities. As they passed, the people from those places would come out to greet them, singing and dancing. Then they would join them and go together to Yerushalayim.

They walked the whole way on foot, singing, dancing and playing musical instruments until they reached Yerushalayim. The Jews came to the Beis HaMikdash and joyously brought their *bikkurim* to the *kohen*. There they thanked Hashem for all the good He had given them — for the good land and good fruit.

Sefer Torah

The *Sefer Torah* is very holy. All of the mitzvos that Hashem commanded us are written in it.

We keep the *Sefer Torah* in a very holy place: in an *aron kodesh* in the shul.

When do we take the *Sefer Torah* out of the *aron kodesh*? During the reading of the Torah.

And when do we read the Torah? On Shabbos, on *Yom Tov*, on Rosh Chodesh and on fast days. We also read the Torah every Monday and Thursday morning.

The Torah is divided up into five *Chumashim*: *Bereishis*, *Shemos*, *Vayikra*, *Bemidbar*, *Devarim*. In each *Chumash*, there are many *parashiyos*.

Every Shabbos we read one *parashah*. Over the whole year, we read all of the *parashiyos* in the Torah.

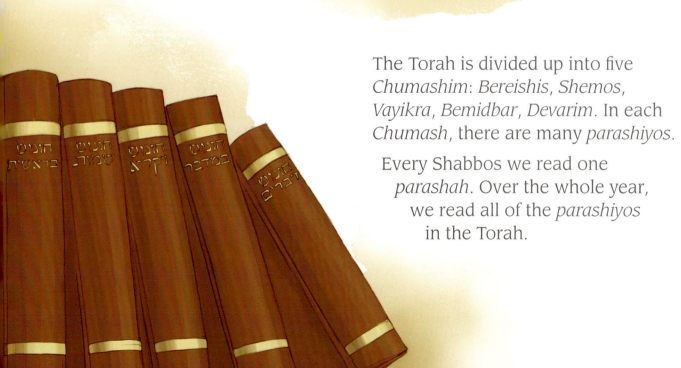

What Did the Sofer Tell Me?

Shmuel the *sofer* lives near my house. He has a special room in his house where he does his work.

I was always curious: What does Shmuel the *sofer* do in his room? What kind of work does he do?

One day while I was playing in the yard, my ball rolled into Shmuel the *sofer*'s yard. I surely didn't want to go into his yard without permission, so I went to the front door and knocked quietly.

"Come in!" I heard the *sofer* say. I opened the door and went inside. Shmuel was sitting near a table and seemed busy with his work.

"Excuse me, I'm sorry," I said. "My ball rolled into your yard."

"Okay, sweet child, wait here for a few minutes," Shmuel said, "because I can't stop my holy work right now." Shmuel sat and wrote while I stood quietly and watched him.

"Have you ever seen how a *Sefer Torah* is written?" he asked me.

"No, I haven't," I answered him. "I'm very happy that I'm getting to watch you now. It's so special and holy!"

The *sofer* smiled and continued to ask me, "Do you know what is written in a *Sefer Torah*?"

"Of course I do! All of the mitzvos of the Torah are written in the *Sefer Torah*. And in shul I hear how they read from the *Sefer Torah*," I answered.

"How wonderful that you listen in shul!" exclaimed the *sofer*. "Soon I will explain to you how one writes a *Sefer Torah*."

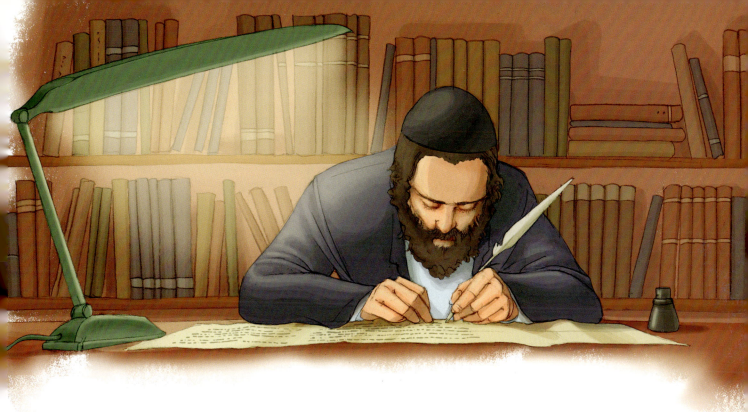

Meanwhile, Shmuel the *sofer* finished writing. He stopped his work and called me to come closer. I looked at the paper that he was writing on and saw that it wasn't paper at all!

"What is a *Sefer Torah* written on?" I asked.

"On sheets of parchment," he answered. "It's called *klaf*. These sheets are made from the skin of a kosher animal. The skin is cleaned very well and processed especially with the intention that it be used for holy Sifrei Torah."

"And what kind of pen do you use to write a *Sefer Torah*?"

"A *Sefer Torah* is written with a special pen called a *kulmos*, made from a goose feather. The end of the feather is sharpened and that's what I dip into the black ink."

I looked carefully at the parchment on the table and at the black shiny letters.

"What beautiful writing!" I said in amazement.

"Yes, this is the special writing for the *Sefer Torah*," answered Shmuel. "Each letter has a special form. And we have to learn a lot in order to know exactly how to write the letters and how to set up the lines. This is very holy work and if, *chalilah*, there is a mistake in the *Sefer Torah*, then it is *pasul*, and it can't be used for the Torah reading in shul.

"A *sofer*'s thoughts must be pure while he is writing," Shmuel added. "When I am writing, I think about the great mitzvah that I am doing. And I daven to Hashem that nothing should go wrong because of me."

"When will you finish writing this *Sefer Torah*?" I asked.

"It will still take a long time. I hope to finish before Shavuos," answered Shmuel.

"And what will you do with the *Sefer Torah* when you're finished?"

"I'll have all the sheets of parchment sewn together. Then I'll have the wooden poles — the *atzei chaim* — attached on both sides. A beautiful cover will be made for it. Then there will be a big celebration and it will be brought to the shul."

"Oh, how exciting! A *hachnasas Sefer Torah*!" I exclaimed.

After Shmuel the *sofer* had explained it all, he opened the door to his yard and gave me back my ball.

"Thank you, thank you!" I said and ran home happily. I couldn't wait for Shavuos.

And then, a few days before Shavuos, I saw a sign. The sign said that there was going to be a *hachnasas Sefer Torah* in our neighborhood!

How happy everyone was! Men, women and also many children participated in the celebration.

At the head of the procession, children marched with torches and lit the way for the *Sefer Torah*. Next were the *Rabbanim* and *talmidei chachamim* walking under a decorated *chuppah* with the beautiful *Sefer Torah*. Then there was a huge crowd of people singing and dancing in honor of the Torah.

שִׂישׂוּ וְשִׂמְחוּ
בְּשִׂמְחַת-הַתּוֹרָה
וּתְנוּ כָּבוֹד לַתּוֹרָה!

Rejoice in the celebration of the Torah, give honor to the Torah!

Torah is More Valuable than Anything

Once upon a time, there was a group of merchants traveling together on a ship to a faraway country. It was a long trip and they passed the time, as merchants do, by talking about their merchandise.

"Mine is the most valuable," claimed one merchant. "I have gold and silver jewelry."

"No, mine is even more valuable," said another. "I have priceless fabric which is made with gold and silver thread."

"My merchandise is more valuable than anyone else's," boasted a third merchant, who held a small chest. "I have precious stones in here. Diamonds and pearls!"

Only one of the passengers, who was a Jewish *talmid chacham*, sat quietly. He was learning Torah.

"What kind of merchandise do you have?" one of the men asked him.

"My merchandise is more valuable than any other," he answered.

"Can you show us what you have?" they asked.

"No, it cannot be seen," he answered.

The merchants searched in every nook and cranny of the ship for the mysterious merchandise. But they didn't find anything. And so, they began to make fun of the Jew and his merchandise.

"Ha, ha, ha! How could you have something that can't be seen?" they ridiculed him.

The Jewish man didn't answer them. He just continued learning.

All of a sudden, pirates raided the ship!

After stealing all the valuable merchandise, they took the penniless passengers to a faraway foreign land.

The merchants had nothing. They had no food, no money, and they didn't know anyone in the city who could help them. They wandered in the streets, hungry, thirsty and very sad.

What do you think the *talmid chacham* did? He went to the *beis midrash* in the city and discussed Torah with the people there. The people saw that he was a great Torah scholar. They took him through the streets of the city with great honor and brought him to the home of the wealthiest man of the town. There he was given good food to eat and whatever else he needed.

The *talmid chacham* didn't forget about the poor merchants. He asked the people of the city to give them food and drink and a place to live.

The merchants were very grateful to the *talmid chacham* for his kindness to them. Now they finally understood the great value of his merchandise. And no robber or misfortune could possibly take it away from him!

What was the Jew's merchandise? It was the Torah knowledge in his head!

כִּי טוֹב סַחְרָהּ – מִכָּל סְחוֹרָה!

For it is more valuable than any merchandise!

A Song about Torah
(to the tune of "*Sameach Te'samach*")

Torah is our one
   and only goal,
Keeping mitzvos
   with our heart and soul,
We'll follow the Torah
   each and every day,
We'll always go
   the precious Torah way.

Different Names for Shavuos

The holiday of Shavuos has many names:
Shavuos, Chag haKatzir, Yom haBikkurim, Atzeres, Zman Matan Torah.

Shavuos: because we count *sefiras ha-omer* for seven weeks (*shivah shavuos*).

Chag haKatzir: because this holiday (*chag*) comes out during the harvest season (the *katzir*).

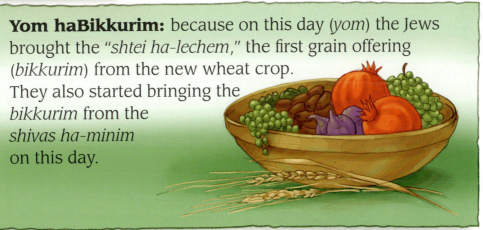

Yom haBikkurim: because on this day (*yom*) the Jews brought the "*shtei ha-lechem*," the first grain offering (*bikkurim*) from the new wheat crop. They also started bringing the *bikkurim* from the *shivas ha-minim* on this day.

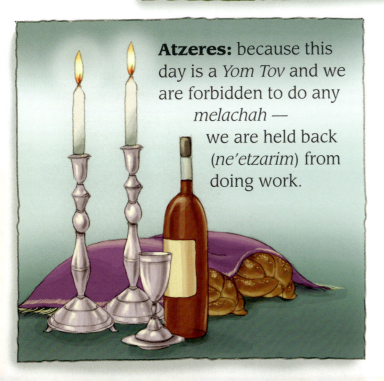

Atzeres: because this day is a *Yom Tov* and we are forbidden to do any *melachah* — we are held back (*ne'etzarim*) from doing work.

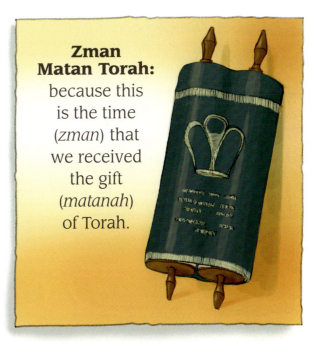

Zman Matan Torah: because this is the time (*zman*) that we received the gift (*matanah*) of Torah.

Megillas Ruth

On Shavuos, The Book of Ruth, *Megillas Ruth*, is read in shul. This is how it begins:

וַיְהִי בִּימֵי שְׁפֹט הַשֹּׁפְטִים, וַיְהִי רָעָב בָּאָרֶץ...

In the days when the *shoftim* judged, there was a famine in the land...

The Story of Megillas Ruth

The story happened many years ago, even before there was a Beis HaMikdash in Yerushalayim.

A wealthy and important man named Elimelech lived in the city of Beis Lechem. Elimelech's wife was a righteous woman, a *tzaddekes*, and her name was Naomi. They had two sons named Machlon and Kilyon.

It was a sad time, because there was a famine in Eretz Yisrael. That means that there wasn't enough food to eat. There was no wheat growing in the fields and no fruit growing on the trees. All the Jews were hungry and sad.

Every day, poor and hungry people came to Elimelech's house and said, "Elimelech, please give us food! We are starving!"

Elimelech thought to himself, "Maybe I should leave Eretz Yisrael and go to a different country where there is no famine." He took his wife and children and they traveled together to the country of Mo'av.

Oh, dear! What had Elimelech done? He had left the holy land of Eretz Yisrael and his Jewish brothers and had gone to live with the non-Jews!

Soon after, Elimelech was punished for what he had done. He lost all of his money and he became very poor. After that, he got sick and died.

Naomi was left alone with her two sons, with no money. Her sons, Machlon and Kilyon, grew up there, in Mo'av, among the non-Jews. Machlon married a non-Jewish woman named Ruth. His brother Kilyon married a non-Jewish woman, too, named Orpah.

Oh, my, what had they done?

Machlon and Kilyon were also punished and they also died. Now Naomi was left all alone, without her husband and children. She was lonely and sad.

One day, Naomi heard that the famine had stopped in Eretz Yisrael — Hashem had pity on His people! Naomi immediately decided to go back to the Holy Land.

She told her daughters-in-law, "I want to go back to Eretz Yisrael. I can't live here among the non-Jews anymore."

Ruth and Orpah were devoted daughters-in-law to Naomi. They loved her and didn't want her to be alone. "We also want to go to Eretz Yisrael," they both said.

Naomi began her trip back to Eretz Yisrael, and Ruth and Orpah went with her. When they got close to Eretz Yisrael, Naomi turned to her daughters-in-law and said, "Go back, my daughters! Go back to your homes! You will have a better life there. Hashem will reward you for all the kindness you have done for me."

"No! We don't want to go back," both Ruth and Orpah said. "We want to go with you to your country and your nation. We want to be with you forever," they begged.

"My dear daughters," Naomi explained, "you can't come with me to Eretz Yisrael. Don't you know that the Jews have many, many mitzvos? How will you keep them? You are both used to living among non-Jews. It's better for you to go home, my daughters."

Orpah listened to Naomi, kissed her goodbye and went back home. But Ruth wouldn't part from Naomi. With all her heart she wanted to be a Jewish woman.

"Look," Naomi said to Ruth, "Orpah has gone home. You should go, too. Your father is the king! In his home you will live a life of comfort and have everything you need. If you stay with me, what will you have? I'm so poor, you won't even have bread to satisfy you!"

"No, Naomi," Ruth answered. "Please don't force me to leave you. I want to be a Jewess like you. I will always feel lucky and happy to be able to keep the mitzvos of the Torah."

Naomi saw that Ruth really meant what she said. She truly wanted to be a Jewess and Naomi didn't try to talk her out of it anymore.

Naomi and Ruth continued walking together to Eretz Yisrael until they finally reached Beis Lechem.

When the women of the city saw Naomi, they were shocked. "Is this Naomi?" they asked. "Is this the rich lady we once knew? She looks so poor now!"

Naomi answered, "Don't call me Naomi, anymore. You can call me Mara, because my life has become bitter." (The word "*mar*" means bitter.) All the women pitied Naomi and felt very sorry for her.

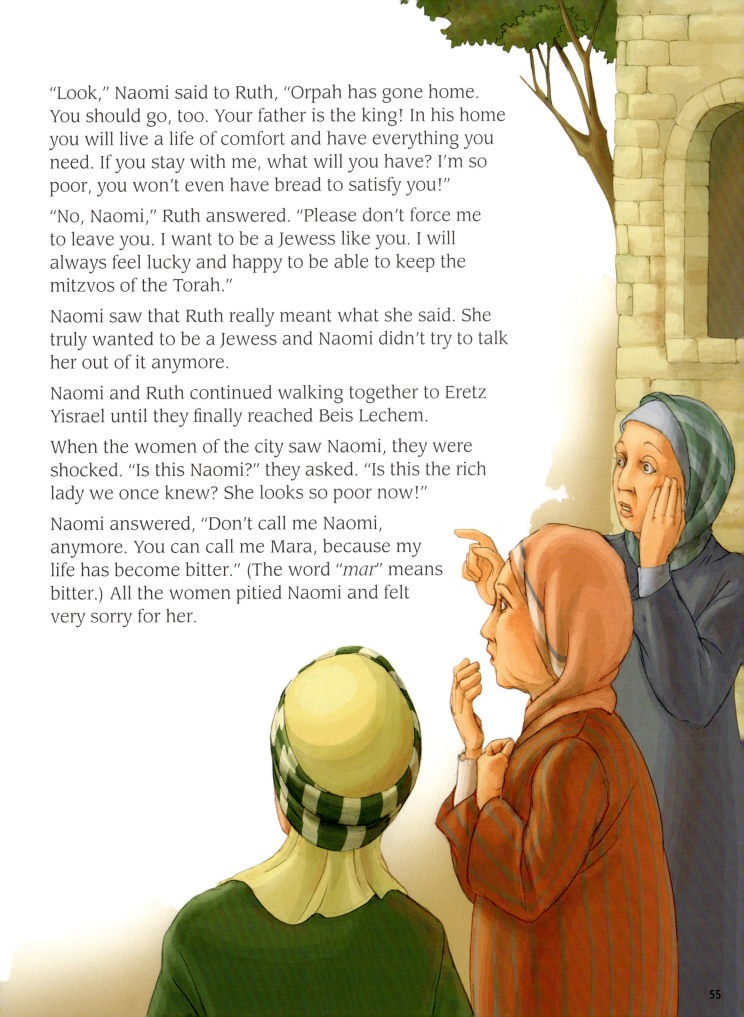

Naomi and Ruth found a place to live. The time of year was the harvest season.

One day Ruth asked Naomi, "Should I go the field to gather some wheat stalks? We have no food left in our house and we are so poor."

"Yes, that's a good idea," Naomi answered. "There is a mitzvah in the Torah for the field owners to leave stalks for the poor people as a present.

"Listen well, my dear Ruth. If you see one or two stalks that fell from the bundle of the harvester, you may take them. According to the Torah, they are 'leket.' But if you see three stalks, don't take them, because they belong to the owner of the field. And there is another mitzvah in the Torah called 'pe'ah.' One corner of the field is not harvested. You may take from this corner. And there is yet another present the Torah gives the poor people. This is called 'shikchah.' If the owner of the field forgot about a whole bundle, the poor people may take it."

Ruth listened carefully to everything that Naomi had told her.

Ruth went on her way. She came to the field of a rich and righteous man named Bo'az. But Ruth didn't know that Bo'az was related to her father-in-law, Elimelech.

Ruth collected wheat stalks in Bo'az's field just as Naomi had taught her.

Bo'az came to the field and greeted his workers.

"May Hashem be with you!" he blessed them.

"May Hashem bless you!" they answered.

Bo'az took a careful look at his workers and noticed a poor girl in the field. He could see that she was wise since she followed all the rules of *leket*, picking up one stalk or two, but not three. He could also see that she was very modest. When she wanted to pick up the stalks, she didn't bend down from her waist. Instead, she bent her knees and that was how she reached the stalks.

"Who is this young woman?" Bo'az asked his workers.

"This is the girl who came back with Naomi from the land of Mo'av," they answered.

When Bo'az heard this, he immediately went over to Ruth and said, "How good it is that you came to my field! From now on, always come here, and do not go to any other field. If you are hungry or thirsty, you will get food and drink from me."

"Why do you want to do this for me?" Ruth asked, surprised.

"I have already heard about all the kindness that you did for your mother-in-law," Bo'az answered. "May Hashem reward you for all of your efforts!"

Ruth did as Bo'az said. When she finished collecting stalks, she ate with Bo'az, making sure to set aside some food for Naomi. Then she gathered up all her stalks, thanked Bo'az and hurried back to Naomi.

She gave Naomi all of the stalks and the food she had saved for her. "Look!" Ruth said to Naomi. "I gathered all of this from one field, the field of a man named Bo'az. He is a good and kind man and he treated me well. He even gave me food to eat."

When Naomi heard this, she was very happy. "Bo'az is our relative," she told Ruth. "He is from Elimelech's family. Hashem was very kind to you by leading you to Bo'az's field. From now on, only go to his field."

Ruth did as she was told. Every day she went to the wheat field of Bo'az, until the end of the harvest season.

Now, listen children, to what happened.

When Bo'az saw how kind and modest Ruth was and how noble her deeds were, he decided to marry her. And the righteous Ruth gave birth to a righteous son. His name was Oved. What joy!

And when Oved grew up, he had a righteous son named Yishai.

And when Yishai grew up, he had a righteous son named David.

When David grew up, he became the king of the Jewish people — he was David HaMelech!

Ruth merited being the grandmother of David HaMelech because of her righteous deeds.

Do you know, children, who David HaMelech was? He was a very great *tzaddik* and understood the Torah very, very well. All day and night he sat and learned Torah. Even when he was king, he continued learning as he was accustomed.

David HaMelech kept a harp next to his bed. At midnight, when a northern wind blew, the harp would begin to play music. When David HaMelech heard the music of the harp, he would immediately get up to thank and praise Hashem. Then he would learn Torah for the rest of the night.

David HaMelech composed the holy book of *Tehillim*. This is a book filled with the prayers and praises that David HaMelech said to Hashem, the Creator.

David was born on Shavuos and also passed away on Shavuos. That is why we read *Megillas Ruth* on this day.

דָּוִד, מֶלֶךְ יִשְׂרָאֵל, חַי וְקַיָּם!
**David, king of Israel,
lives and remains forever.**

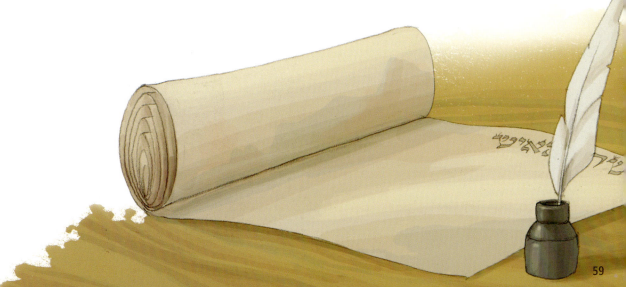

Summer Fruits

Summer is here — how happy all the children are!

The fruits on the trees are ripe and ready to be eaten. Yossi's mother gave him a new fruit today. How nice it looks and how good it smells!

"A peach!" Yossi called out happily. "It looks so tasty. Thank you, Imma!"

Imma smiled and said, "Yossi, do you know how to thank Hashem for the new fruits?"

"For sure!" answered Yossi. "First, I'll say the *berachah*, *borei pri ha-etz*."

"Yes, that's right," said Imma. "But there is also another *berachah*, a special *berachah* that we say for new things, such as a new fruit, new clothing, and even a new mitzvah!"

"Yes, now I remember!" Yossi said proudly. "The *berachah* of *she'hecheyanu*.

Yossi held the fruit in his hand. He joyfully said the *berachah* of *borei pri ha-etz* and the *berachah* of *she'hecheyanu*. Then he ate the sweet fruit.

For every new fruit of the season we joyfully say,

בָּרוּךְ אַתָּה... שֶׁהֶחֱיָנוּ וְקִיְּמָנוּ וְהִגִּיעָנוּ לַזְּמַן הַזֶּה.

Blessed are You...Who has kept us alive and sustained us and enabled us to reach this season.

Riddles

One of the *shivas ha-minim*
I'm proud to be,
And your kiddush cup is filled
With juice from me!

Which fruit am I?

Sometimes sour,
Sometimes sweet,
Dark red and small,
I'm a super special treat!

Which fruit am I?

Orange and small,
And mostly round,
My pits you collect,
For a game on the ground!

Which fruit am I?

With hundreds of seeds,
And a nice little crown,
On Rosh Hashanah you'll find me,
All over your town!

Which fruit am I?

Peel me and cook me,
For a sweet, crunchy taste,
Not even one kernel,
Will you want to waste!

Which "fruit" am I?

Filled with black pits,
I'm like a green ball,
Everyone likes me,
Whether big or small!

Which fruit am I?

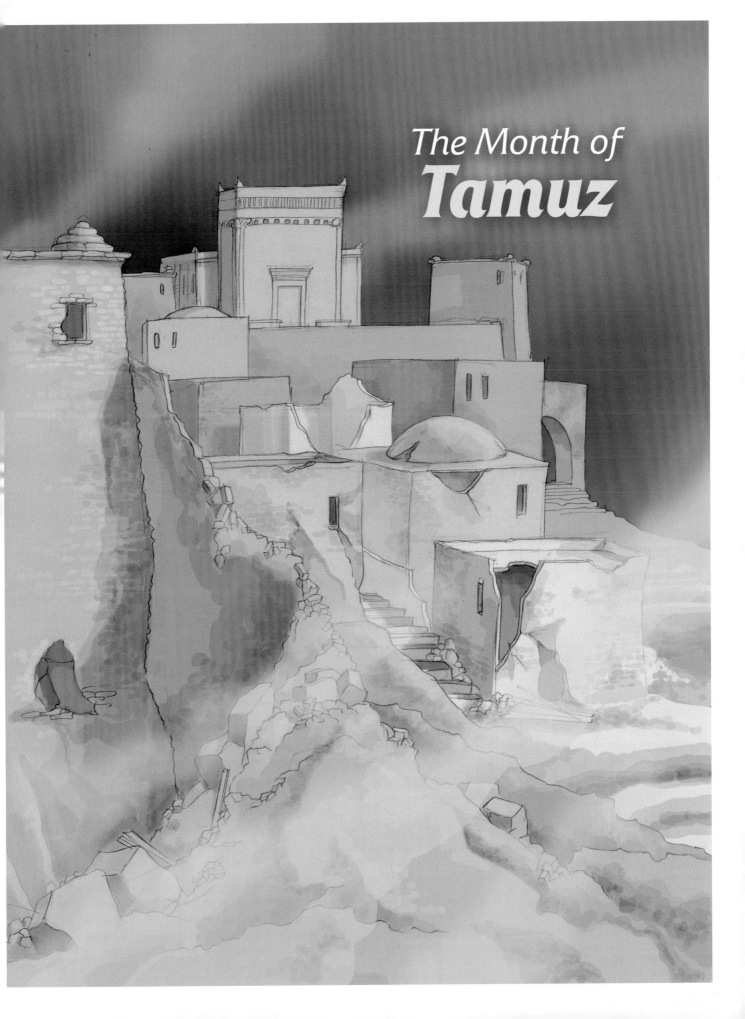

The Month of Tamuz

The Three Weeks

During the warm summer days, while the flowers are in bloom and the children are happily playing, we have three sad weeks.

What happened? Why are we suddenly sad? During these days, we are sad about our beautiful Beis HaMikdash that was burned down. We are also sad about all the troubles the Jews had and that we went into *galus*.

These days are called "*bein ha-metzarim*," or the Three Weeks. Why?

We call these days *bein ha-metzarim* because they are the sad days between two days of sorrow (*tzarah*) — the seventeenth day of Tamuz and the ninth day of Av. On the seventeenth day of Tamuz, the wall around Yerushalayim was broken into and on the ninth day of Av, the Beis HaMikdash was burned.

During these three weeks, we don't play music, we don't get haircuts and we don't make weddings. We think about how good it was when we had our Beis HaMikdash and we pray to Hashem that He rebuild it.

יִבָּנֶה הַמִּקְדָּשׁ, עִיר צִיּוֹן תְּמַלֵּא.

**May the Beis HaMikdash be built,
the city of Tziyon refilled.**

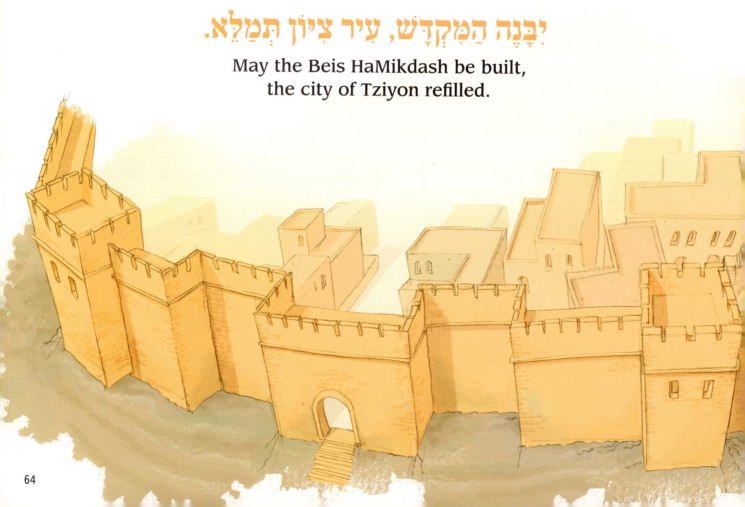

Yerushalayim in Her Glory

How beautiful and glorious,
Was our special city.
When the Beis HaMikdash stood,
So pure and pretty.

The *Kohanim* and *Levi'im*,
Served Hashem each day.
"Please rebuild it again!"
We hope and we pray.

Oh, what a wonderful sight it was to see Yerushalayim all built up in the days when the Beis HaMikdash was so magnificent. People came from far and near to see the beautiful Beis HaMikdash. Chazal said, "Anyone who did not see the Beis HaMikdash, has never seen a beautiful building."

But the true beauty of the Beis HaMikdash was that it was the holiest and purest place in the world. Hashem's Presence was there; He was so close to the Jewish people!

When a Jew had a question or a request, he would come to the Beis HaMikdash. He would ask for what he needed and would leave happy and content.

If, *chas v'chalilah*, a Jew sinned and felt bad about what he had done, he would come to the Beis HaMikdash. He would bring a *korban* to Hashem and repent for what he had done — he did *teshuvah*. The sacrifice atoned for his sin and Hashem forgave him.

The service of the *Kohanim* and *Levi'im* was an amazing sight to see!

The *Kohanim* were dressed in special clothing. They brought sacrifices on the *mizbe'ach* and lit the golden menorah. They did all kinds of holy work, using the special *keilim* of the Beis HaMikdash.

The *Levi'im* played special musical instruments and sang songs of praise. They also guarded the Beis HaMikdash.

The *Kohen Gadol* had special, holy tasks. He wore eight special garments, some made with gold!

The *Kohen Gadol* wore the *choshen* over his heart. The *choshen* had twelve precious stones which glittered and shone with different colors. On each stone was the name of one of the *shevatim* of the Jewish people. Inside the *choshen*, were the holy *urim v'tumim*. The Jewish people were able to ask a question and get an answer from Hashem through the *urim v'tumim*. The letters on the *choshen* would light up and the *Kohen Gadol* would understand Hashem's answer from the letters. Then he would explain it to the one who asked.

Oh, how special it all was!

The *Kohen Gadol* wore the holy *tzitz* on his forehead. It was made of pure gold and it glittered and shone. The words, "*kodesh laHashem*" were on the *tzitz*. Whoever looked at the *tzitz* would do *teshuvah* right away!

He also wore an *ephod* and a special *me'il* made of blue *techeles*. On the hem of the *me'il* were golden bells and woolen "pomegranates." When the *Kohen Gadol* went into the Beis HaMikdash, the sound of the tinkling bells was heard.

What a magnificent sight it was to see the *Kohen Gadol* on *Yom Kippur*! He wore special white clothing and went into the *Kodesh haKodashim*, where he did a special *Yom Kippur Avodah*. He purified himself, sacrificed *korbanos*, and prayed and asked Hashem to forgive all the Jewish people.

How great was the happiness on the *Shalosh Regalim* when all of *Klal Yisrael* went up to the Beis HaMikdash in Yerushalayim. Hashem took special care of the Jews, just like a good father takes care of his children, and He did many miracles for them.

There was a special place,
With always plenty space.
Jews came from far away,
They all had room to stay.

The Beis HaMikdash was the place,
Where everyone had space!

Oh, the Jews had it so good then! When they all learned Torah and did mitzvos, they were all healthy and happy; there were no problems and no suffering! There was blessing in everything they did — their fields grew nicely and the fruits were big, tasty and healthy.

Everything — oh, everything! — was successful and prosperous.

And so, the Jews were able to relax and learn Torah; they enjoyed peace, tranquility and happiness. Also, the non-Jews gave them a lot of respect. They saw that Hashem loves His nation and protects them.

Oh, how beautiful and glorious Yerushalayim was!

But because of our sins, we don't have a Beis HaMikdash anymore.

*We've lost
our special place,
Oh, what a disgrace!*

The Seventeenth Day of Tamuz

Shivah Asar b'Tamuz is a fast day. It is a sad day for us, because many misfortunes happened on this day.

Many years ago, in the wonderful times when the Beis HaMikdash was still standing, something terrible happened. The Jews stopped keeping the mitzvos and they began to bow down to idols. Hashem sent righteous prophets (*nevi'im*) to tell the Jews to do *teshuvah*.

The *nevi'im* came to the Jews and said, "Dear Jews! Do *teshuvah*! Return from your evil ways for your own good. If you continue what you are doing, *goyim* will come from far away and there will be a great tragedy!"

But the Jews didn't listen to the *nevi'im*. They continued doing bad deeds.

Hashem waited many years for the Jews to return to Him and do *teshuvah*. Hashem has tremendous patience and He has pity on all. He doesn't want to give punishment. He told the *nevi'im* to go back — again and again — and tell the Jews to do *teshuvah*. Maybe, just maybe, it would help.

But no, *Klal Yisrael* continued doing bad deeds, until one day Hashem gave them a terrible punishment…

The *goyim* came from far away to fight the Jews. But they couldn't get into Yerushalayim because there was a very big, strong wall surrounding the city.

The *goyim* made a siege around Yerushalayim. They put many soldiers all around the wall and didn't allow the Jews to go in or come out of the city. The Jews couldn't bring food from the fields around Yerushalayim. Soon, there was a terrible famine in Yerushalayim — there was no food to eat!

How terrible it was for *Klal Yisrael*! The soldiers stood around the wall for a very long time. They wanted to break the wall but they couldn't.

Why not? Because Hashem was still giving the Jews a chance! He was waiting for them to do *teshuvah*. And if they did, they would win over the *goyim* and would be able to chase them away from Yerushalayim!

But the Jews didn't return to Hashem. And then…
on the seventeenth day of Tamuz, the *goyim* broke
the wall and entered Yerushalayim. Oh, how terrible it was!

They killed many, many Jews. For three weeks they made the Jews suffer terribly. And then on the ninth day of Av, they burned down the Beis HaMikdash.

The seventeenth day of Tamuz, the sad day that the *goyim* broke the wall of Yerushalayim, was made into a fast day for all generations. On this day, we say *selichos* and ask Hashem to forgive us and rebuild the Beis HaMikdash.

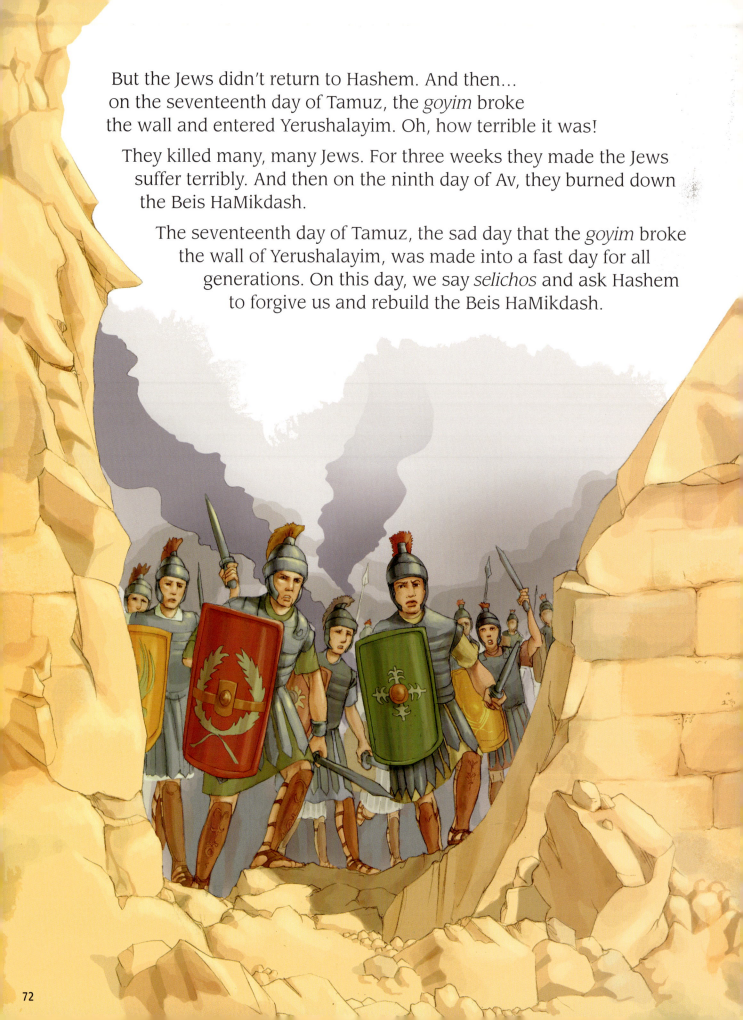

The Nine Days

מִשֶּׁנִּכְנַס אָב - מְמַעֲטִים בְּשִׂמְחָה!

Once Av begins, we lessen our joy.

When the month of Av begins — the month in which the Beis HaMikdash was destroyed — we are very sad.

During the nine days between Rosh Chodesh Av and Tishah b'Av, we don't drink wine or eat meat during the weekdays. We don't bathe, or wash clothing, or wear freshly washed clothing. We cut down on activities that bring us happiness.

The Ninth Day of Av

The saddest day of the year is Tishah b'Av. This is the day that our precious Beis HaMikdash was destroyed. It is the greatest and most awesome tragedy in all of Jewish history.

Tishah b'Av is a fast day. On this day we are extremely sad and mournful and so we don't eat, don't drink, don't wash and don't wear leather shoes.

On the night of Tishah b'Av, we turn on only a few lights, since light brings happiness, and it is not a time for joy.

In shul, we turn over the benches and chairs. We sit on or close to the floor and daven *Ma'ariv* in a sad tune. After the davening, we read *Megillas Eichah* and we say *kinnos*. These are sad poems *(piyutim)* for crying and mourning about the destruction of the Beis HaMikdash.

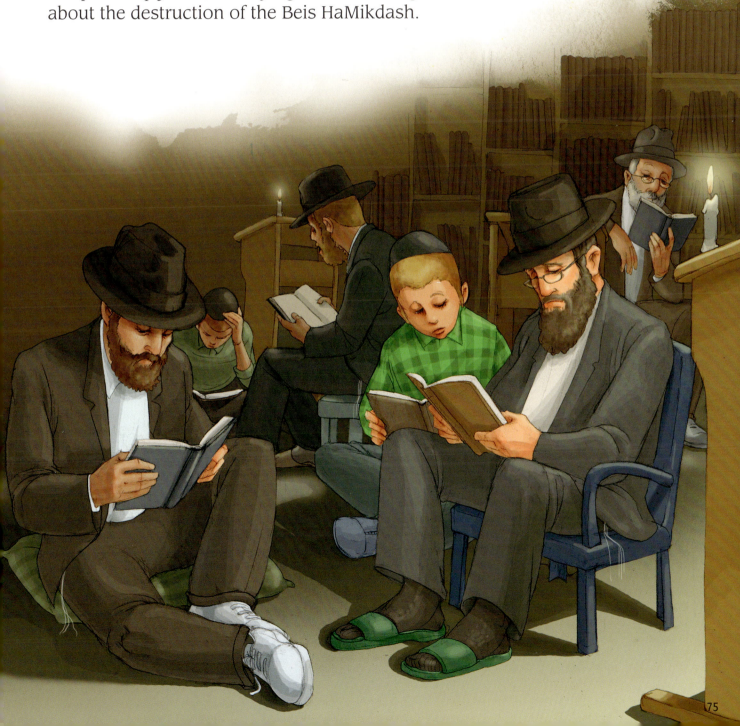

Tishah b'Av

Oh, Yerushalayim, the city we love!
A tragedy befell on Tishah b'Av.
Oh, Yerushalayim, we cry for you!
We wait till you are built anew.

Oh, what can we do, what can we say?
We want the Mikdash rebuilt today!
If we are kind and we are good,
It will stand again just as it should!

Every mitzvah, every deed,
Adds a brick, we will succeed!
Every Jew can do his part,
And build the Mikdash
  with all his heart!

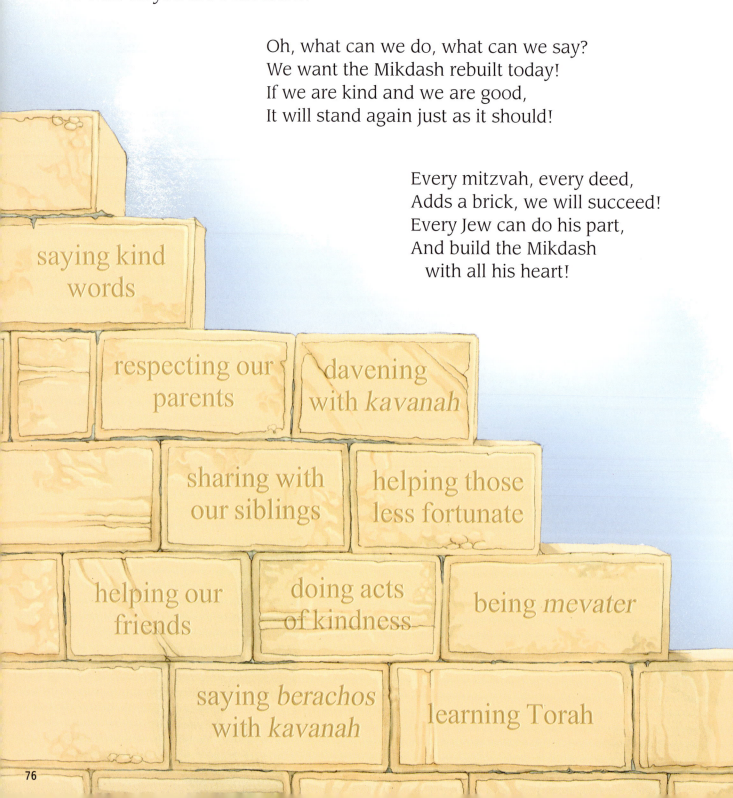

saying kind words

respecting our parents

davening with *kavanah*

sharing with our siblings

helping those less fortunate

helping our friends

doing acts of kindness

being *mevater*

saying *berachos* with *kavanah*

learning Torah

Megillas Eichah

What is *Megillas Eichah*?

Megillas Eichah was written by the *navi*, Yirmeyahu. Yirmeyahu lived during the time of the destruction of the Beis HaMikdash. Beforehand, he warned *Klal Yisrael* many times and told them to do *teshuvah*. When the Jews didn't listen to him, and even made fun of him, he didn't get angry at them. He had pity on them and asked them over and over to behave better.

When Yirmeyahu saw the destruction of the Beis HaMikdash and the suffering of *Klal Yisrael* as they went into *galus*, he sat and cried. Then he wrote *Megillas Eichah*, which is all about the suffering of the Jews during that time.

At the end of *Eichah*, Yirmeyahu wrote,

הֲשִׁיבֵנוּ הַשֵּׁם אֵלֶיךָ וְנָשׁוּבָה חַדֵּשׁ יָמֵינוּ כְּקֶדֶם.

Bring us back to You, Hashem, and we will return; renew our days as they were in the past.

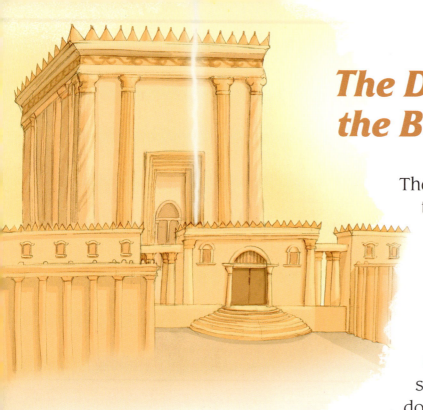

The Destruction of the Beis HaMikdash

The story of the destruction of the Beis HaMidkash is so sad. The destruction happened twice and both times it was on Tishah b'Av.

Why was it destroyed?

During the first Beis HaMikdash, the Jews did bad deeds. They served *avodah zarah* and bowed down to idols. Hashem sent them many warnings through the *nevi'im*, but they didn't listen. And then this sad day came, the day the Beis HaMikdash was destroyed.

After that, the Jews did *teshuvah*. Hashem forgave them and brought them back to Eretz Yisrael. They were able to build the Beis HaMikdash again!

But — oh, how sad it was! — years passed and the Jews again left the ways of Torah. Once more something terrible happened. The second Beis HaMikdash was also destroyed!

Why was it destroyed?

Because of *sinas chinam* — insults and revenge. During the time that the second Beis HaMikdash stood, the Jews did not treat each other nicely. There was hatred among the people — arguments, fights, terrible *lashon ha-ra* and people didn't want to make peace.

Listen to what happened in Yerushalayim during the time of the second Beis HaMikdash.

Kamtza and Bar Kamtza

There was a very rich man living in Yerushalayim in a big, beautiful house. One day he made a huge party. He invited all his friends as well as the *Rabbanim* and *talmidei chachamim* of Yerushalayim.

One of the people he wanted to invite was Kamtza, his good friend, and he sent a messenger to invite him. But what happened? The messenger made a mistake! Instead of inviting Kamtza, he invited someone else whose name was Bar Kamtza. He had no idea that Bar Kamtza was not a friend; he was actually the rich man's enemy!

When Bar Kamtza heard that he was invited to the party, he was very surprised. He thought, "Why am I being invited? Maybe the rich man wants to make up with me."

Bar Kamtza got all dressed up for the party and went to the rich man's house. He sat with all of the other guests — the rich man's friends. When the rich man came over to greet his guests, whom did he see? Bar Kamtza, his enemy!

"What are you doing here?" he shouted. "We are enemies, why did you come?"

Bar Kamtza was very embarrassed. His face became very pale.

"There must have been a mistake," Bar Kamtza said. "But now that I'm here, please don't chase me out. Don't embarrass me! I will pay you for whatever I eat and drink," he begged.

"No, absolutely not!" the rich man said in anger. "Get out right now!"

"I will pay you half of the cost of this whole party," Bar Kamtza offered. "Just don't embarrass me!"

"No, I don't agree! Get out now!" the rich man thundered.

"I will pay you for the whole party," Bar Kamtza said in desperation. "Just don't send me away!"

"No! Get out! Just get out!" the rich man answered. And he grabbed Bar Kamtza and threw him out of the house.

Bar Kamtza left and was very, very angry at the rich man. He should have forgiven him; that would have been the right thing to do because an argument is never good. But instead of forgiving him, he wanted to get back at him. He thought to himself, "The rich man embarrassed me in front of everyone at the party. And no one even stopped him! Even the *Rabbanim* and *chachamim* — no one said a word! They must have agreed with what he did.

"I'm going to show them all," he thought. "They're going to pay for what they did! The Roman king will come to fight them and burn down their houses."

Bar Kamtza didn't realize that what he was about to do was a very bad idea. He was so angry that he decided to speak badly about the Jews to the king. He wanted the king to punish *Klal Yisrael*, but he should have realized this was a big *aveirah*. Besides, wasn't he also a Jew? His house would be burned down together with the others. He, too, would suffer! But he was too angry to think things through.

Bar Kamtza went to the Roman king and said, "The Jews are rebelling against you! They don't want you to be their king."

"How do I know that what you are saying is true?" asked the king.

Bar Kamtza answered, "Send an animal to the Beis HaMikdash. If the Jews sacrifice it, you will know that they are loyal to you, but if they don't, then you will know that they hate you."

The king did as Bar Kamtza suggested and sent a calf as a sacrifice.

On the way to Yerushalayim, Bar Kamtza did something very tricky — he cut the calf's lip. He knew that the *Kohanim* wouldn't sacrifice the calf if he had a blemish, a *mum*, since this wasn't allowed!

When Bar Kamtza reached Yerushalayim, he gave the king's calf to the *Kohanim*. And what happened? They checked it and found the cut on its lip. So of course they couldn't bring it as a sacrifice.

Bar Kamtza went back to the Roman king and told him the Jews didn't want to sacrifice his calf. The king got very angry and sent his cruel general, Titus, with a big army to fight the Jews. There was a big war.

The Jews tried to fight the Romans and stop them from entering Yerushalayim. But because of their *aveiros*, they didn't succeed. The Romans kept advancing until they reached the Beis HaMikdash on the seventh day of Av.

Oh, how terrible! The wicked Romans went into our holy Beis HaMikdash. They destroyed and demolished everything. They put out the flames of the menorah and they broke the *mizbe'ach*. The evil Titus took the beautiful *paroches* and made a bag out of it. He took all of the *keilim* of the Beis HaMikdash, put them inside and took them for himself. He wanted to show them off and boast about how he had defeated the Jews. The Romans stayed there and laughed and made fun of the Jews while they ruined everything in the Beis HaMikdash.

On the ninth day of Av, they lit the Beis HaMikdash on fire. Oh, how terrible! This is how our holy, precious Beis HaMikdash — the joy of our lives — was destroyed.

Ever since the Beis HaMikdash was destroyed, the Jews haven't had peace. For all these generations we have had a lot of problems and suffering.

We daven to Hashem to take us out of the bitter *galus* and build the third Beis HaMikdash quickly.

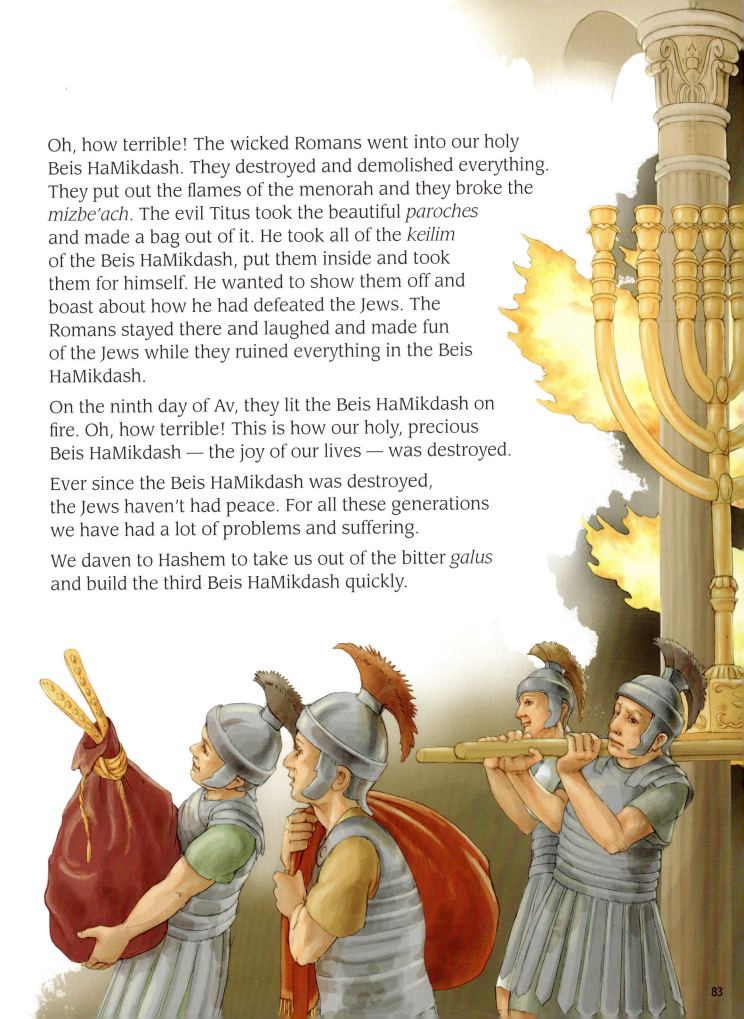

What happened to the evil Titus?

He traveled by boat back to Rome. Suddenly there was a big storm and the ship was in danger of sinking. Titus called out, "The God of the Jews can only punish with water. He punished Pharoah with water, he punished Noach's generation with the flood. If He is really all-powerful, let Him fight with me on dry land. Then we'll see who will win!"

A *bas kol* came from *shamayim* and said, "You evil man! I have a little creature in the world called a *yatush*, a mosquito. It is small and weak; let's see if you can win over it!"

The storm immediately stopped and the ship continued on its way.

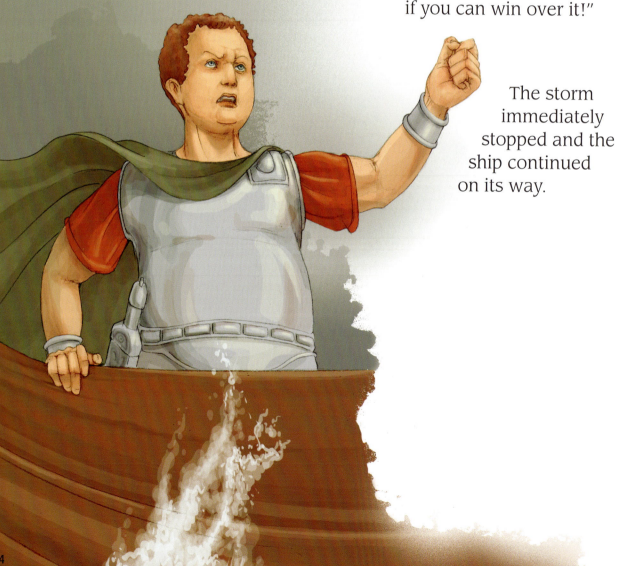

When Titus reached Rome, all the Romans came to honor him. He showed off the *keilim* of the Beis HaMikdash that he had stolen and told them all about his victories over the Jews. While he was still bragging, a tiny little mosquito flew right into his nose!

Titus tried to get the mosquito out, but he couldn't. The mosquito went deep into his head and gnawed at his brain.

"Oh, it hurts!" cried Titus. "My head hurts me so much!"

The mosquito continued to gnaw at his brain for a long time. Finally Titus died in great pain. This is how Hashem punished Titus, who was so arrogant: A tiny little mosquito defeated him!

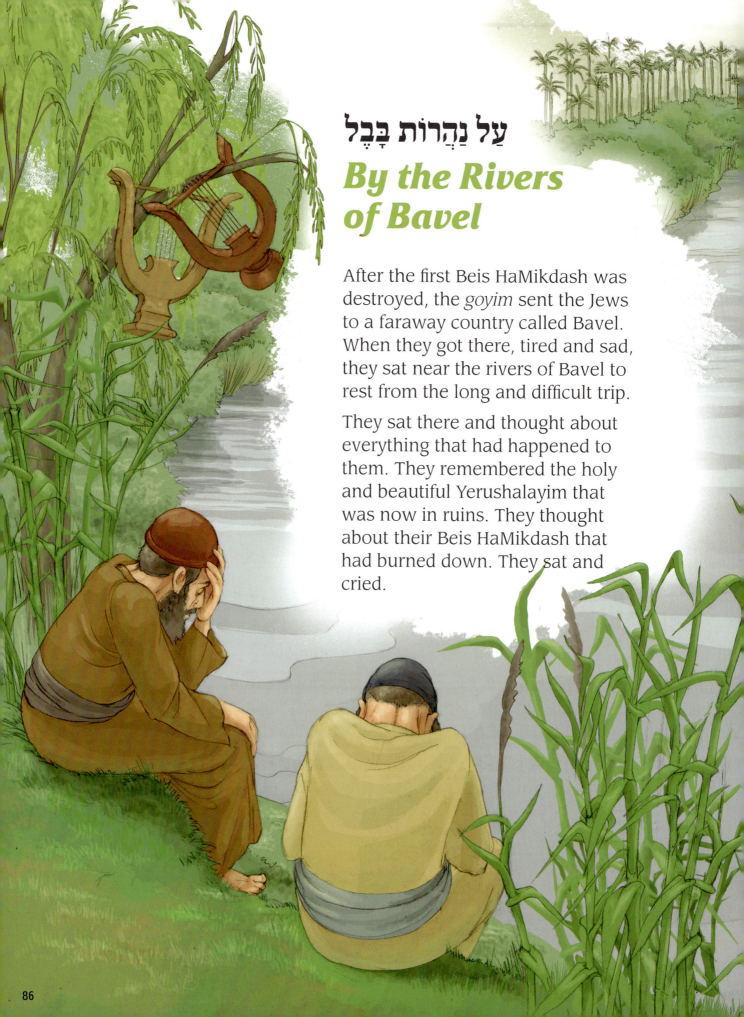

עַל נַהֲרוֹת בָּבֶל
By the Rivers of Bavel

After the first Beis HaMikdash was destroyed, the *goyim* sent the Jews to a faraway country called Bavel. When they got there, tired and sad, they sat near the rivers of Bavel to rest from the long and difficult trip.

They sat there and thought about everything that had happened to them. They remembered the holy and beautiful Yerushalayim that was now in ruins. They thought about their Beis HaMikdash that had burned down. They sat and cried.

The wicked *goyim* came over to them and said, "Sing us a song from Tziyon! Sing us one of the beautiful songs that you sang in the Beis HaMikdash!"

The sad Jews answered, "How can we sing the song of Hashem? How can we sing those holy songs here, in the land of the *goyim*?"

Right then and there the Jews promised each other that they would always remember Yerushalayim, no matter where they would be.

אִם־אֶשְׁכָּחֵךְ יְרוּשָׁלַיִם תִּשְׁכַּח יְמִינִי — If I forget you, Yerushalayim, may my right hand forget its skill.

They promised to remember Yerushalayim at every happy occasion.

אַעֲלֶה אֶת יְרוּשָׁלַיִם עַל רֹאשׁ שִׂמְחָתִי — I will make mention of Yerushalayim at the beginning of my happiness.

Because as long as Yerushalayim is not rebuilt with a Beis HaMikdash, our happiness is not complete.

A Reminder of the Destruction

We remember Yerushalayim at all times, and mourn the destruction of the Beis HaMikdash. Whenever we have a *simchah*, we do something to help us remember.

At a wedding, the *chassan* breaks a glass under the *chuppah*. When we paint a house, we leave one area unpainted. We call this *"zecher l'churban,"* a reminder of the destruction.

When will our happiness be complete? When the Beis HaMikdash is rebuilt.

כָּל הַמִּתְאַבֵּל עַל יְרוּשָׁלַיִם זוֹכֶה וְרוֹאֶה בְּשִׂמְחָתָהּ!

Whoever mourns Yerushalayim, will merit to see its joy!

The Western Wall

The Beis HaMikdash is no more,
But there's one remaining wall.
No! Hashem didn't let it burn,
It stands so strong and tall!

Jews come from everywhere,
From countries far away.
To *Avinu ba-shamayim*,
We speak our hearts and pray.

Only one wall was left from the Beis HaMikdash; Hashem didn't allow the Romans to destroy it. This wall is the Western Wall, the *Kosel HaMa'aravi*.

The *Shechinah*, the Presence of Hashem, has never left this holy place. That is why Jews come from all over the world to pray there. Everyone asks Hashem to have pity on us and build us a Beis HaMikdash once again.

רַחֵם בְּחַסְדְּךָ, עַל עַמְּךָ - צוּרֵנוּ!
עַל צִיּוֹן מִשְׁכַּן כְּבוֹדֶךָ -
זְבוּל בֵּית תִּפְאַרְתֵּנוּ!
בֶּן-דָּוִד עַבְדְּךָ יָבוֹא וְיִגְאָלֵנוּ,
רוּחַ אַפֵּנוּ, מְשִׁיחַ הַשֵּׁם!

Our Rock, have mercy in Your kindness,
upon Your nation, on Tziyon, the place of Your
glory, home of Your splendor. Son of David,
Your servant, should come and redeem us,
our very breath, Mashiach of Hashem.

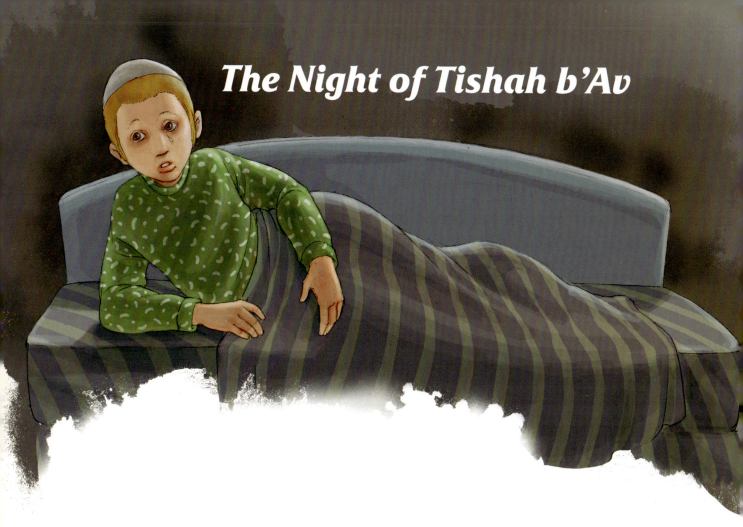

The Night of Tishah b'Av

Darkness… night… the night of Tishah b'Av.

All the children are sleeping, only Yossi can't sleep. He's lying on his bed, looking around and trying to keep his eyes closed. He just can't fall asleep.

He feels so very sad. He thinks and thinks…

"Oh, what a sad day it is today! The holy Beis HaMikdash was destroyed today. We have no *Kohanim*, we have no *Levi'im*, we have no *korbanos*, we have so much suffering… The Jews have so many troubles in *galus*! Hashem, please help us!"

These were Yossi's thoughts. He didn't even realize that he had started crying.

"What's the matter, Yossele?" Imma said worriedly as she came into his room. "Why are you crying? Does something hurt you?"

"No, Imma. Nothing hurts," Yossi answered. "I'm just sad, very sad that we don't have the Beis HaMikdash. I can't help crying."

"Oh, my Yossi, my dear Yossi! Your tears are so precious. HaKadosh Baruch Hu loves you and will listen to your *tefillos*! He will send the Mashiach speedily in our days!"

Yossi heard what his mother said and calmed down. His heart filled with hope and anticipation for the coming of Mashiach and the rebuilding of the Beis HaMikdash.

"Oh, how good it will be," he thought. Slowly his eyes closed and he fell asleep.

In the morning when the sun rose, Yossi opened his eyes and called his mother. "Imma, Imma! I had a dream! All the Jews did *teshuvah* and the *geulah* came!"

Imma kissed him on the forehead and said, "My dear Yossi, you dreamed a wonderful dream. I hope we will be *zocheh* to it soon!"

Waiting for the Geulah

We are always waiting for the *geulah*. Three times a day in *Shemoneh Esrei* we beg Hashem, "יְהִי רָצוֹן... שֶׁיִּבָּנֶה בֵּית-הַמִּקְדָּשׁ — May it be Your will, Hashem... that the Beis HaMikdash be rebuilt."

We also mention the Beis HaMikdash in *Birkas haMazon*. "וּבְנֵה יְרוּשָׁלַיִם, עִיר הַקֹּדֶשׁ, בִּמְהֵרָה בְיָמֵינוּ — Rebuild Yerushalayim, the holy city, speedily in our days".

We always remember the Beis HaMikdash and wait for Mashiach to come.

> יִבָּנֶה הַמִּקְדָּשׁ עִיר צִיּוֹן תְּמַלֵּא,
> וְשָׁם נָשִׁיר שִׁיר חָדָשׁ וּבִרְנָנָה נַעֲלֶה...

May the Beis HaMikdash be rebuilt, the city of Tziyon You shall fill, and there we shall sing a new song, and with song we will go up...

The Mashiach's shofar, we will hear,
We'll run towards him, when he comes near!
We'll sing and dance in Shabbos clothes,
We'll greet Mashiach, eyes aglow!
We'll beat the drums and thank Hashem,
For all the *nissim*, once again!

The Coming of Mashiach

Children, do you know how wonderful it will be when Mashiach comes and rebuilds the Beis HaMikdash?

It will be just like during the time when we left Mitzrayim. We were like princes and Hashem, our King, did so many miracles for us. When Mashiach comes, we will also see many miracles.

All of the nations will respect the Jews and will be afraid to harm them. The Jews will come from all over the world to Eretz Yisrael. From the four corners of the earth all the Jews will be gathered and brought to the Holy Land.

Oh, how good and happy those days will be — everybody will be healthy and there won't be any troubles or suffering!

There will be peace in the world. Even the wild animals will be peaceful. Wolves will live with lambs, and leopards with goats.

Oh, how good and successful everything will be then for the Jews. The fields will grow wonderful crops and the fruits on the trees will be big and tasty!

Most important, there will be true happiness. All people will be good and will only want to do good things. There will be holiness and purity everywhere. The Jews will live peacefully and happily, and will be able to sit and learn Torah. Oh, how wonderful it will be at the time of the *geulah* when Mashiach comes, may it come speedily in our days.

אֲנִי מַאֲמִין, אֲנִי מַאֲמִין,
בֶּאֱמוּנָה שְׁלֵמָה בְּבִיאַת הַמָּשִׁיחַ.
וְאַף־עַל־פִּי שֶׁיִּתְמַהְמֵהַּ, עִם כָּל זֶה
אֲחַכֶּה לוֹ בְּכָל יוֹם - שֶׁיָּבוֹא! אֲנִי מַאֲמִין!

I believe with perfect faith
in the coming of Mashiach.
And even though he may tarry,
I still will wait for him each day to arrive.
I believe! I believe!

Shabbos Nachamu

The Shabbos after Tishah b'Av is called Shabbos Nachamu. On this Shabbos, we read the *haftarah* that begins with the words, "*Nachamu, nachamu ami* — Be comforted, be comforted, my nation." In this *haftarah*, Hashem comforts (*menachem*) the Jews after the destruction of the Beis HaMikdash and promises them that he will redeem them if they do *teshuvah*. For this reason, the whole month of Av is called "Menachem Av."

Tu b'Av

The fifteenth day of Av is called Tu b'Av. It is a happy day, since many happy things happened to the Jews on this day.

Chazal say, "The Jewish people never had a day as happy as Tu b'Av."

Glossary

Aron kodesh: the repository in which the Torah scrolls are kept in a synagogue.

Aseres haDibros: the Ten Commandments.

Aveiros: sins.

Avodah: the service performed in the Beis HaMikdash.

Avodah zarah: idol-worship.

Bas kol: a voice from Heaven.

Beis din: a Jewish court of law.

Beis midrash: a "house of Jewish learning" where men gather to study.

Berachah: a blessing.

Bikkurim: [the offering of] the first fruits.

Birkas haMazon: the Grace after Meals.

Chalilah: "God forbid!"

Chametz: leavened foods, prohibited during Passover.

Chas v'chalilah: "God forbid!"

Chassan: a bridegroom.

Chessed: acts of kindness.

Choshen: the breastplate worn for the Temple service.

Chumash (pl. Chumashim): [one of] the Five Books of Moses.

Chuppah: lit., "the wedding canopy"; the wedding ceremony.

Daven: pray.

Ephod: an apron-like garment worn during the Temple service.

Erev: lit., "evening"; the day preceding a Sabbath or Festival.

Galus: exile from the Land of Israel.

Geulah: redemption.

Goyim: non-Jews.

Hachnasas Sefer Torah: celebration of the completion of a new Torah scroll.

Hadassim: myrtle branches.

Haftarah: a passage from the Prophetic writings.

Hakadosh Baruch Hu: the Holy One, Blessed be He.

Har: a mountain.

Kavanah: concentration or devotion during prayer.

Keilim: holy vessels used in the Holy Temple.

Kinnos: dirges recited on Tishah b'Av.

Klal Yisrael: the Jewish people.

Kodesh haKodashim: the Holy of Holies, the most inner room of the Beis HaMikdash.

Kohen (pl. Kohanim): member(s) of the priestly tribe.

Kohen Gadol: the High Priest.

Korban (pl. korbanos): an offering or sacrifice brought in the Holy Temple.

Korban ha-omer: the Omer-offering, brought on the 16th day of Nisan.

Korban Pesach: the Pesach-offering.

Lashon ha-ra:	derogatory or harmful speech about another person, forbidden by the Torah.
Levi'im:	Levites, members of the tribe of Levi.
Ma'ariv:	the evening prayer service.
Mashiach:	the Messiah.
Matan Torah:	the giving of the Torah on Mount Sinai.
Me'il:	the outer garment worn by the *Kohen Gadol*.
Melachah:	a labor forbidden by the Torah on the Sabbath and Festivals.
Mevater:	to accede.
Nissim:	miracles.
Parashah (pl. parashiyos):	the weekly Torah portion.
Paroches:	the curtain in front of the Holy Ark.
Pasul:	unfit; invalid.
Rabbanim:	rabbis.
Sefer:	a holy book.
Sefer Torah (pl. Sifrei Torah):	Torah scroll(s).
Sefirah:	the forty-nine days between Pesach and Shavuos.
Sefiras haOmer:	the counting of the forty-nine days between Passover and Shavuos.
Selichos:	special penitential prayers.
Shalosh Regalim:	the three pilgrimage Festivals: Sukkos, Pesach and Shavuos.
Shamayim:	Heaven; the sky.
Shemoneh Esrei:	lit., "eighteen"; the blessings of the Amidah prayer, which forms the main part of the prayer service.
Shevatim:	the twelve tribes of Israel.
Shivas ha-minim:	the seven species with which the Land of Israel is blessed.
Simchah:	a joyous occasion.
Sinas chinam:	unfounded hatred.
Sofer:	a scribe.
Talmidei chachamim:	Torah scholars.
Tamei:	ritually impure.
Tanna (pl. Tanna'im):	Sage(s) of the Mishnah.
Techeles:	wool dyed sky blue.
Tefillos:	prayers.
Teshuvah:	repentance.
Tzaddik (pl. tzaddikim):	a righteous, holy person.
Tzitz:	the golden plate worn on the *Kohen Gadol*'s forehead.
Urim v'tumim:	a priestly device for communicating with God.
Yiras shamayim:	fear of Heaven.
Yom Tov:	a Jewish holiday or Festival.
Zocheh:	to merit.

Coming soon!

Check your favorite bookstore for upcoming volumes of Round and Round the Jewish Year:

Elul-Tishrei and **Adar-Nisan**